LIFELINES

PRE-INTERMEDIATE

STUDENT'S BOOK

D1205742

TOM HUTCHINSON

OXFORD UNIVERSITY PRESS

Contents

Unit	Grammar	Vocabulary	Reading
Getting started **p6**	Questions p6	Introduction p7	
Everyday life **p8**	**Routines** The present simple tense p8	Collocations p10	**Nature's children** **Language focus:** *should/shouldn't* p10
Appearances **p16**	**People-watching** The present continuous tense (v present simple) p16	Physical appearance p18	**Lonely hearts** **Vocabulary file:** Describing people **Language focus:** *have/have got* p19
Life stories **p24**	**Gretna scene** The past simple tense: regular and irregular endings p24	Money p26	**The Witch of Wall Street** **Language focus:** *so ... that ...* p26
The future **p32**	**A night out in London** *will;* first conditional p32	Country adjectives p34	**The end of the melting pot?** p34
Comparisons **p40**	**General knowledge quiz** Comparatives and superlatives p40	Clothes **Language focus:** Clothes with plural names p44	**Eye to eye** **Language focus:** *as ... as ...* p42
People and places **p48**	**An embarrassing incident** The past continuous tense (v past simple) p48	Places and buildings p52	**The roof of the world** **Vocabulary file:** Descriptive adjectives and adverbs p50
In your life **p56**	**Have you ever ...?** The present perfect tense (v past simple) p56	Homophones and homonyms p58	**Where are they now?** **Language focus:** The present perfect with *for/since* p58

Listening and Speaking	Pronunciation	Extension	Writing (Workbook)
Telling the time p12	The IPA p13	Reading and listening: **Facts of life** p14	Linking words (1): *and, but, or* WB p10
Making arrangements **Language focus:** time prepositions; present continuous (future) **Conversation pieces:** Making arrangements p20	Voiced and voiceless consonants Question intonation p21	Listening and speaking: **Talking about your family** **Vocabulary file:** Families p22	Personal letters WB p15
Telling your life story **Conversation pieces:** Life events p28	*-ed* ending Word stress with two syllables p29	Reading and listening: **Shark Attack!** **Language focus:** Adverbs and adjectives p30	Linking words (2): *because, so, although* WB p21
Messages **Conversation pieces:** Leaving messages **Language focus:** *will* for spontaneous decisions p36	/ɪ/, /i:/ Sentence stress p37	Reading and listening: **South for the winter** **Vocabulary file:** Transport p38	Messages WB p26
In a clothes shop **Language focus:** *too/enough* **Conversation pieces:** Shopping p45	/ɒ/, /ɔ:/ Reduced vowels p46	Listening and speaking: **You've got what it takes** (song) p46	Reference (1): pronouns and possessive adjectives WB p31
Asking the way **Language focus:** Giving directions p52	*-a-* Word stress with three syllables p53	Reading and listening: **It was a normal day ...** **Language focus:** Participles as adjectives p54	Narratives WB p37
Meeting visitors p60	/θ/, /ð/ Auxiliary verbs: strong and weak forms p61	Reading and listening: **Two brothers** p62	Formal letters WB p42

Contents

Unit	Grammar	Vocabulary	Reading
Food and health **p64**	**The pyramid** Countables and uncountables; *some* and *any* p64	Food and drink p65	**The Big Man** **Vocabulary file:** Quantities **Language focus:** *used to* p66
Possibilities **p72**	**How honest are you?** *would*; second conditional p72	Crime p74	**Would you get involved?** p74
Activities **p80**	**The New Year's Resolution** *going to* (v *will*) p80	Gerunds; activities p82	**The £349 housewife** **Vocabulary file:** Work p82
The media **p88**	**Image** *have to/can*: past and future p88	The media p90	**Fiona's new look** **Language focus:** *want someone to …* p90
Planet Earth **p96**	**The rubbish dump in the sky** The passive p96	The natural world p98	**Comet!** p98
Time **p104**	**The forgotten years** The past perfect tense p104	Time expressions p106	**Body clock** **Language focus:** Nouns used as adjectives p106
Work **p112**	**Managing your time** Tense revision p112	Adjectives and nouns p114	**Heroic, brave or just crazy?** p114
	Reflecting on Learning p120	Grammar Reference p122	Tapescripts p132

Listening and Speaking	Pronunciation	Extension	Writing (Workbook)
In a restaurant **Conversation pieces:** Ordering a meal p68	Silent letters Sentence stress p69	Reading and listening: **How long could you live?** p70	Reference (2): *this, these, it, they* WB p47
Checking into a hotel **Conversation pieces:** Polite requests p76	*-ou-* Emphatic stress p77	Reading and listening: **Smart shopping** p78	Filling in a form WB p53
Making suggestions **Conversation pieces:** Expressions with *-ing* forms p84	/tʃ/, /ʃ/ Making suggestions p85	Listening and speaking: **The pleasure principle** p86	Postcards WB p58
Getting through **Conversation pieces:** Telephone expressions p92	Consonant clusters List intonation p93	Reading and listening: **Gladiators!** p94	Describing and explaining WB p63
Oh, really? p100	/ə/ Word linking (1) p101	Reading and listening: **Going for gold** p102	Formal and informal letters WB p69
Arranging a time **Conversation pieces:** Arranging a time p108	*-u-* Word linking (2) p109	Reading and listening: **The strange story of Martin Guerre** p110	Text linkers WB p74
Small talk **Conversation pieces:** Small talk p116	Revision p117	Reading and listening: **Summertime Blues** (song) p118	Revision: A newsletter WB p79
Word list p140	Irregular verb list / IPA chart (inside back cover)		

Getting started

Grammar
Questions

1 Read about Gianni.

a Work with a partner. What information do you think is missing from the text?

Hi. My name's Gianni. I'm from _____ and I'm 26 years old. I'm studying English because I need it _____ . I work _____ . I learnt English at _____ and at _____ , too. But I've forgotten a lot of it. I think that my biggest problem with English is _____ . People speak very _____ and I can't _____ them. But I like English. I can talk to people _____ , and I can understand the _____ of _____ , too.

b 📼 *0.1* Listen to the conversation and check your ideas.

c Complete the text.

2 Can you remember Mary's questions?

a Write the questions.

b 📼 *0.1* Listen and check.

c Think of two more questions that Mary could ask.

3 Find out about someone in the class.

a Ask and answer the questions from **2** with your partner.

b Work in a group of four. Introduce your partner to the group, telling them what you found out.

4 Write a paragraph to introduce yourself, using Gianni's text in 1 as a model. Add extra information if you want.

➤ See **Reflecting on Learning 1**: Your aims p120.

5 Look at the letters of the alphabet.

a Practise saying the alphabet.

A B C D E F G H I J K L M N O P Q R S T U V W X Y Z

b 📼 *0.2* Listen, check and repeat.

6 You will hear a conversation.

a Look at the form and answer these questions.
  1 Who do you think is speaking?
  2 What is the conversation about?
  3 What questions do you expect?

Car insurance

For a free quotation, phone

AA

Insurance

Freephone 0800 444777

Name:

Mr / Mrs / Miss / Ms
(delete as appropriate)

Surname [_____]

First name(s) [_____]

[_____]

male ☐   female ☐

Address:

Number [_____]

Street [_____]

Town/city [_____]

County [_____]

Postcode [_____]

Tel no:

Area code [_____]

Number [_____]

Occupation [_____]

[_____]

Age last birthday [_____]

Vehicle:

Make/Model [_____]

[_____]

b 📼 *0.3* Listen and check your ideas.

c 📼 *0.3* Listen again and complete the form.

7 Interview your partner and complete the form with your partner's information.

Vocabulary
Introduction

1 Match these questions and possible replies.
Some have more than one answer.

What does *look up* mean?	It's called a *pencil sharpener*.
How do you say *armario* in English?	It means *find the word in a dictionary*.
What's this called in English?	We say *cupboard*.
How do you spell *married*?	I'm sorry. I don't know.
Can you repeat that, please?	It's spelt M-A-double R-I-E-D.
How do you pronounce this word?	Yes, of course. M-A-double R-I-E-D.

2 **Look at the picture.**

a Label as many things as possible.

b Work in groups. Compare your ideas, using the expressions in **1**.
Can you now label any more things?

3 **Test your memory.**

a Close your book.

b ▭ *0.4* Listen and answer the questions.

➤ See **Reflecting on Learning 2**: Recording vocabulary p120.

1 Everyday life

Grammar
The present simple tense

Grammar in use

1 Read the text and answer these questions.
1 Why do we have routines?
2 Who describes her routine?
3 Are routines good or bad?

Routines

Think about your daily life. Do you follow the same route to work every day? Do you sit in the same place in class? When you get dressed, do you always put the same leg or arm in first? You probably do, because we all have routines in our lives.

Routines save time and energy because you do them without thinking. That's why they are so important in the morning when your brain isn't very active. Here's Jo talking about her morning routine.

'Oh yes, I always do exactly the same things. I wake up at seven o'clock every morning, but I don't get up till quarter past seven. I switch on the radio and listen to the news. Then I go to the loo and I brush my teeth. I have a shower and dry my hair. Then I choose my clothes and I get dressed. I don't eat anything for breakfast. I just have a cup of coffee. Then I go to work. Yes, it's always the same.'

Routines are very useful, but they also make you uncreative. So sometimes it's a good idea to break your routines. Get out of bed on the opposite side. Listen to a different radio station. Take a different route to work. Eat something different for breakfast. Change your routine. You never know, it could change your life.

2 Work with a partner. Discuss these questions.
1 How is your morning routine different from Jo's?
2 What other routines do you have in your life?

Rules

1 Look at the table.

a Complete the second column, using *She*.

I	She
I always do exactly the same things. I wake up at seven o'clock. I don't get up till quarter past seven. I switch on the radio. I listen to the news. I go to the loo. I brush my teeth. I have a shower. I dry my hair. I choose my clothes. I get dressed. I don't have any breakfast.	*She always …*

b 🔊 *1.1* Listen and check.

2 Look at your table from 1.

a What normally happens to the verb in the third person singular?

b What happens
  * when the verb ends in *-se*, *-sh*, *-ch*, e.g. *brush*? How do we pronounce these words?
  * when the verb ends in *-o*, e.g. *go*?
  * when the verb ends in consonant +*y*, e.g. *dry*?
  * with the verb *have*?

3 How do we make negatives and questions in the present simple tense
  * for the third person singular?
  * for all other subjects?

4 When do we use the present simple tense?

a These two sentences illustrate the two main uses of the present simple tense.

I wake up at seven o'clock every morning.
Routines save time and energy.

b Complete the rule using two of these phrases:

- things that are happening at the moment
- things that happen regularly
- general truths

We use the present simple tense to describe _____
_____ and _____ .

➤ Check the rules for the present simple tense in **Grammar Reference 1.1**.

Practice

1 Ken shares a flat with three friends. He describes their morning routine.

a Put the verbs in the box in the correct form to complete the text. Some are in the negative. Use some more than once.

turn up   like   come down   miss   watch   stay   have   get up
hurry   listen to   go   wake up   switch on   run   take   start

Christine _____ first at about seven o'clock. She _____ downstairs and _____ breakfast early, because she _____ work at eight o'clock. When I _____ , I _____ the radio and _____ the news. Then I _____ and _____ a shower. I _____ downstairs at about quarter past seven. Sam _____ at about half past seven. She _____ _____ the radio, so she _____ the television and _____ the breakfast programme. She always _____ the volume too loud, so we usually _____ an argument about that. Colin _____ to college and he's always late. He _____ usually _____ breakfast. He _____ downstairs at the last minute, and _____ out to get the bus. But he usually _____ it, so then I _____ him in my car and I'm late for work. I _____ the weekends, because everyone _____ in bed late. But I _____ _____ in bed. I _____ first and _____ my breakfast in peace!

b 🔊 *1.2* Listen and check.

2 These questions are from an interview with Ken.

a Only four questions are correct. Correct the other questions.
  1 Have you a shower every morning?
  2 Do you listen to the radio in the morning?
  3 What time you go downstairs?
  4 Why do you likes the weekend?
  5 When do your flatmates get up?
  6 Does Christine get up first at the weekends?
  7 Do Sam listen to the radio?
  8 What programme she watches?
  9 How does Colin get to college?
  10 Does he often misses the bus?

b Roleplay the interview with a partner.

c Ask your partner questions about a typical morning in his/her home.

3 How compatible are you with other people?

a Write down
- a kind of music that you like and a kind that you don't like.
- your favourite food and something that you don't eat.
- your favourite drink and something that you don't drink.
- a game or sport that you play and one that you don't play.
- a TV programme that you always watch and one that you don't watch.
- something that you always do in the morning and something that you don't do.
- something that you often read and something that you don't read.

b Talk to other people in the class, using these expressions.
  *A I don't like jazz. **Do you?***
  B Yes, I do, but I don't like opera.
  What about you?
  *A No, I don't like opera **either**.*

c Who has the same likes and dislikes as you? Tell the class.

d Tell the class some of the other things that you found out.
  EXAMPLES
  Mario doesn't drink milk.
  Carla doesn't read the newspapers.

➤ Look at **Reflecting on Learning 3**: Parts of speech p120.

Vocabulary
Collocations

1 **Here are some verb phrases that go with the noun *bed*.**

make a
buy a
get out of *salir*
go to   bed
get into *metete*
lie in *tirado*
stay in
have breakfast in

a Write down some verb phrases for each noun in this list. You can use a dictionary to help you.

house
home
school
work
holiday
car
bus
television

b Compare your phrases with the class.

2 **Look at your list of activities.**

a Find things that you
- do every day.
- only do at weekends.
- never do.
- do in the evenings.
- sometimes do.
- would like to do.
- don't want to do.

b Compare your ideas with a partner.

➤ See **Reflecting on Learning 4**: Using dictionaries p120.

Reading
Nature's children

1 **Look at the photographs from the article.**

a Read the first paragraph and discuss these questions.
1 Who are these people?
2 What kind of lifestyle do you think they have?
3 What do they do?

b Read the rest of the article and check your ideas.

c How does the writer feel about these people?

Nature's children

It's summer and the New Age Travellers are here again. In their vans, old buses and caravans, they move from place to place. Angry MPs, farmers and local people appear on television and complain about them: 'The police shouldn't allow it! They should put them all in the army!' etc., etc.

The Travellers don't have jobs, because they don't stay in one place long enough. They are the children of nature – modern gypsies. When autumn comes, they disappear and we don't see them on the news any more. In fact, they move to the cities and look for empty houses for the winter. Perhaps the children go to school for a few months.

Paul and Janice are Travellers. They aren't married. They have two children called Moonstone and Saffron. Their life is very simple. During the day they sit and talk to their friends while the children play. In the evenings they usually eat together with other families around a big fire, and somebody usually plays a guitar or switches on a CD player. They live on social security benefits. If they need extra money, Janice makes jewellery and sells it at markets and fairs.

Both Paul and Janice come from normal middle class families. That's one reason why Paul prefers the life of a Traveller. As Paul explains, '*My father works in an office. He catches the same train to work every day. He comes home at 5.30. And why does he do it? To pay the mortgage on the house. But then what does he do in his free time? He works! He decorates the house, he digs the garden, and he washes the car. He thinks he's free, but he's really just a slave. Well, I don't want to be like that.*'

What should we do about the Travellers? They're rebels against respectable society and they don't care what we think. But why shouldn't they do their own thing? As I sit here at my desk and think about my mortgage, the insurance, and taxes, I wonder who's right.

2 Mark these sentences *True* (✓), *False* (✗) or *Don't Know* (?).

1 New Age Travellers are only
  on the news in the summer. ✓
2 Farmers don't like the Travellers. ☐
3 They spend the winter in
  caravans. ☐
4 New Age children never go to
  school. ☐
5 Janice is Paul's wife. ☐
6 Paul's father works for an
  insurance company. ☐
7 Paul admires his father. ☐
8 Janice doesn't eat meat. ☐
9 Paul makes jewellery. ☐
10 The writer has got a mortgage. ☐

3 Compare Paul's and his father's lifestyles.

a Find expressions in the text that describe each lifestyle and
  complete the chart.

Paul's lifestyle	His father's lifestyle

b Can you add more words and expressions to the chart?

c What do you think about the New Age Travellers? Which lifestyle
  do you find more attractive? Why?

Language focus: *should/shouldn't*

a Complete these sentences from the text.

  The police _____ allow it!

  They _____ put them all in the army!

  What _____ we do about the Travellers?

  But why _____ they do their own thing?

b When do we use *should/shouldn't*?

➤ Check the rules for *should/shouldn't* in **Grammar Reference 1.2**.

c Here are some more opinions about the Travellers. Complete the
  sentences with *should* or *shouldn't*.

'They can do what they like. But why _____ I pay for it? Their
social security benefits come out of my taxes. We _____ pay
them to do nothing.'

'Maybe they don't do any harm. But that's not the point. It's my
land and they _____ be here.'

'It's terrible. The music is so loud and they look so dirty. And the
children! They _____ be at school.'

'People only complain because they're jealous. Every society needs
its rebels. We _____ leave them alone.'

'Well, I don't understand it. He comes from a good home. We're
respectable people. He _____ live like that.'

'We don't do any harm. Why _____ we live the way we want
to? It's a free country.'

'Freedom? Huh. They're just lazy. They _____ get jobs. And if
they don't, we _____ put them in prison or in the army.'

d 📼 *1.3* Listen and check.

---

4 Look at the opinions above.

a Who do you think might express each opinion?

b Which opinions do you agree with?

5 Does your country have groups of people like the New Age
   Travellers? What do they do? How do you feel about them?

Listening and speaking
Telling the time

1 **How do we tell the time?**

a Complete the diagram.

b We can also tell the time in digital form.

EXAMPLES

7:43	*seven forty-three*
13:25	*thirteen twenty-five*
18:00	*eighteen hundred*
8:04	*eight oh four*

o'clock

five past

ten to

quarter past

twenty to

twenty-five past

half _____

2 **Look at these clocks and watches.**

a Say the times.

b 🔲 *1.4* Listen and match the sentences and times.

1 What's the time? ☐
2 What time is our meeting tomorrow? ☐
3 When does the programme start? ☐
4 Excuse me. What time does the next train leave? ☐
5 You're listening to Radio West. ☐
6 Good morning. This is your wake-up call. ☐
7 Could I reserve a table for this evening, please? ☐
8 Could I make an appointment with Dr Clark, please? ☐
9 Could I book a taxi to the airport, please? ☐

a

b

c

d

e

f

g

h

i

3 **Look at tapescript 1.4.**

a Practise the conversations with a partner.

b Make more conversations to
- reserve a restaurant table.
- book a taxi.
- give someone a wake-up call.
- find out the departure and arrival times of a train.
- make an appointment at the dentist's.
- ask when a TV programme starts and finishes.

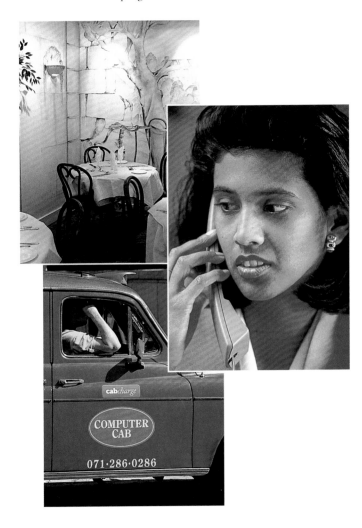

'Remind me – am I getting up or going to bed?'

Pronunciation
The IPA

The International Phonetic Alphabet (IPA) consists of symbols that show *sounds*. These can help you with pronunciation. Often English spelling and English pronunciation are not the same. This is why learning the sound symbols can be very useful for students of English. There is a chart of the IPA symbols on the inside back cover.

1 Vowels

a Say these words and look at the spelling. What do you notice?

b**e**d /e/
h**ea**d /e/
any /e/

These words have *different* vowel spellings but the *same* vowel sound.

b Now say these words and look at the spelling.

h**ea**d /e/
t**ea** /iː/
h**ea**r /iə/

These words have the *same* vowel spelling but *different* vowel sounds.

➤ Look at the IPA chart and study the vowel symbols.

2 Consonants

a Most of the phonetic symbols for consonants are the same as the letters.

big /bɪg/
red /red/

b But some consonant sounds have special symbols.

/ʃ/	**sh**oe	/ʒ/	mea**s**ure
/tʃ/	**ch**air	/dʒ/	**j**ust
/θ/	**th**ing	/ð/	wi**th**
/ŋ/	so**ng**	/j/	**y**es

c Say these words.

/ðiːz/	/rɪtʃ/	/ʃiː/
/θɪŋk/	/sɪŋ/	/jɪə/
/ˈpleʒə/	/brɪdʒ/	/waɪ/

➤ Look at the IPA chart and study the consonant symbols.
You will practise the IPA symbols in this course.

Extension: Reading and listening
Facts of life

1 How do we say large numbers?

a Say these numbers.

> 200
> 2,000
> 2,000,000
> 2,000,000,000

Note that they do not end in *-s*.

EXAMPLES

200 two hundred   6,000 six thousand

b Say these numbers.

> 15,000,000
> 85,900
> 4,000,000,000
> 7,650,300

2 Look at the text. What do you think the missing numbers are?

a Practise saying these numbers.

18	50	100,000,000	22,500,000	100
73,000,000,000	75	591	13,640,872	
1,000	11	22	9,300	157	916,500

b Work with a partner. Complete the text with the numbers in **a**.

c Discuss your ideas with the class.

3 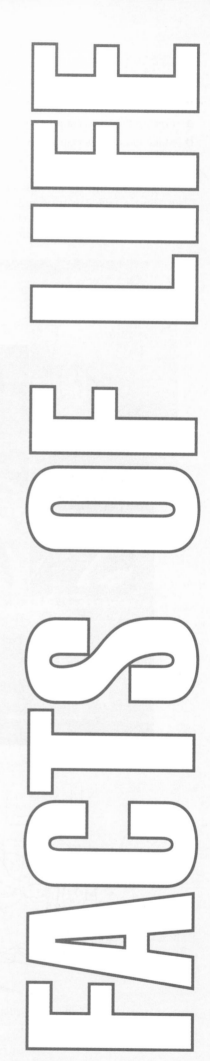 1.5 Listen and check. How many numbers did you guess correctly?

4 Read the text again. Mark these sentences *True* (✓) or *False* (✗).

1 Every hour about 5,700 people die. ☐
2 You spend about 30% of your life asleep. ☐
3 You blink approximately two million times a year. ☐
4 McDonalds sell 916,500 hamburgers in one hour. ☐
5 There are nineteen countries where people drink more alcohol than Britain. ☐
6 Approximately 500 planes take off every hour. ☐

5 In the text find expressions which mean the same as
- approximately *(four possibilities)*.
- more than.
- every day.
- to produce.
- to go up.
- each person.
- a minute.
- a bicycle.

6 Which of the facts in the text do you think are
- the most surprising?
- the most interesting?
- the most depressing?
- the most pleasing?
- the least interesting?
- the most useful?

➤ See **Reflecting on Learning 5**: Making mistakes p120.

Coca-Cola, Coke and the design of the contour bottle are registered trademarks of the Coca-Cola Company

Every hour nearly 15,000 babies are born. The world's population increases by _____, and the world spends over $_____ on weapons.

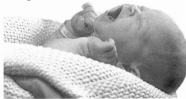

In a lifetime of 65 years the average person watches television for twelve years, and sleeps for almost _____ years.

Your heart beats approximately _____ times in a minute. In that same 60 seconds you breathe in about _____ times and you blink seventeen times. You lose between 50 and _____ hairs and more than a litre of sweat daily.

In one hour the world drinks _____ cans of Coca-Cola. McDonald's hamburger shops serve _____ customers. People buy enough BIC ballpoint pens to draw a line round the equator 160 times.

In one year people in Britain drink _____ cups of tea. Per head they eat 65 loaves of bread and _____ eggs. Each person drinks 216 pints of milk, _____ bottles of wine and 207 pints of beer. But Britain is only twentieth in the league of alcohol drinking countries.

In one hour Volkswagen makes 166 cars at its factory in Wolfsburg, Germany. In the same period of time the Hero Bicycle Company of India produces _____ bikes and the Reynolds Tobacco Company in the United States produces _____ cigarettes.

Every hour over _____ planes take off or land somewhere in the world, and there are _____ recorded earthquakes.

2 Appearances

Grammar
The present continuous tense

Grammar in use

1 Describe the scene. Which tense must you use and why?

2 📼 *2.1* **Read and listen to the text.**

a Answer the questions.
1 Who is speaking?
2 Who is he watching?
3 Who does he think they are?

b Now discuss these questions.
1 Why does the man suspect them?
2 Why does he change his mind?
3 What do you think is really happening?

I often travel to other countries, so I spend a lot of time at airports. Today I'm travelling to Greece and at the moment I'm waiting for my plane. But I'm not wasting my time. What am I doing? I'm playing my favourite game – people-watching. Whenever I have the time, I watch other people.

Take that couple, for example. They're buying magazines at the moment. Are they going on holiday or are they travelling on business? They aren't wearing business clothes, but he's carrying a briefcase. Every few seconds she looks round. Is someone following them? Perhaps they're running away and … Just a minute, there's a story in this newspaper. A bank clerk stole one million pounds last week and disappeared with his wife. There's a picture of them here. Hmmm, they look similar. That's it! The money's in the briefcase. I must stop them.

They're going to the departure lounge now. Quick. Oh, just a minute. They're saying goodbye to each other. The woman isn't going into the departure lounge. She's walking away. Oh well, it was exciting for a moment. Oh, what is she doing now? She's talking to another man. They're kissing. Now, I wonder …

Rules

1 Look at the story again.

a Underline examples of the present continuous tense with *I*, *they*, and *she*. For each of them, find
- a positive statement.
- a negative statement.
- a question.

b How do we make each of these forms?

2 Look at the first paragraph again.

a Two different present tenses are used. Underline examples of each.

b What is each tense? Why is each tense used?

➤ Check the rules for the present continuous tense in **Grammar Reference 2.1**.

Practice

1 Test your partner's memory.

a Write three true and three false statements about the picture, using the present continuous tense.

EXAMPLES

The woman at the newsagent's is carrying a briefcase.
Three men are standing and talking.

b Read out your sentences. Your partner must tell you if they are true or false, without looking at the picture.

2 Choose someone in the picture. Your partner must ask Yes/No questions to find out who it is.

EXAMPLE

A Are you thinking of just one person?
B Yes.
A Is the person male?
B No.
A So, it's a woman. Is she standing up?
B Yes, she is.
A Is she buying something?

3 Look at the text.

a Put the verbs in brackets into the correct present tense.

I _____ (work) for a construction company. We _____ (build) roads, dams, bridges and things like that. At the moment my company _____ (produce) a plan for a new motorway. I usually _____ (work) in the roads department, but this month I _____ (work) in the department that _____ (build) bridges. So my whole working day is different just now. I normally _____ (spend) a lot of time outdoors, because I _____ (go) to the construction sites. But with this new project I _____ (spend) a lot of time in the workshop. At the moment we _____ (test) a model of one of the new bridges. I _____ (enjoy) it a lot, because I _____ (learn) a lot of new things.

b 📼 *2.2* Listen and check.

c Write about your job or studies. Say what you normally do, and what you are doing at the moment.

d Work with a partner. Tell your partner about your job or studies, and answer your partner's questions.

4 Imagine you are people-watching.

a Choose one or two more people from the picture.

b Write a story about them, using this format:
- What do they do?
- Where do they live?
- Why are they at the airport?
- What evidence is there for your story?

➤ See **Reflecting on Learning 6**: Nouns p120.

Vocabulary
Physical appearance

1 **Look at this list of words for describing physical appearance.**

> thin tall fair short wavy green
> handsome fat long young
> dark brown good-looking thick
> red straight big black bald
> pretty blue curly slim grey
> small attractive old well-built

a Work in pairs or groups. Organize the words into four different categories. Some words can belong to more than one category.

b Compare your categories with the class.

c Which of the words do we normally only use for men or for women?

2 **Look at the photographs.**

a Read this description and decide who it is.

> She's quite small and slim. She's got fair hair and blue eyes. Her hair is short and curly.

b Describe the other people, using words from the list.

c Which of the words didn't you use for any of the photos?

d Describe yourself.

Reading
Lonely hearts

1 Look at the adverts.

a Match the adverts and photos.

b Which person would you most like to meet and why?

1

● I'M A SINCERE AND EASY-GOING MAN AND I NEED A LOVING PARTNER. I can cook, iron, and wash up. I have my own house and my own business. I'm 6 feet tall, good-looking and friendly. Surely there's an attractive, intelligent female out there for me? If you're under 35, call **TONY**.

2

● IF YOU'RE OLD AND BORING, DON'T BOTHER WITH THIS AD. I'm looking for a fit and good-looking guy with an exciting lifestyle. I'm a lively, long-haired 23-year-old and I love to have a good time. My interests are tennis, hang-gliding, and discos. Please send a photograph. **MONICA.**

3

● A SOCIABLE AND OUTGOING MALE, 30, WANTS A FUN-LOVING AND ATTRACTIVE FEMALE. Tall or short, dark or fair, I don't care, but you must have a good sense of humour. And you must like dogs. I've got two! Call **DEREK.**

4

● HI. I'M HANNAH. I'm divorced and I've got two children. I'm in my early forties, with blonde hair and blue eyes. Are you a quiet, responsible man about the same age? You must be a non-smoker.

5

● ARE YOU LIKE ME? ARE YOU 17–20? ARE YOU SHY? Do you sit at home in the evenings with nothing to do? Is your best friend a computer? Please write to me. I'd love to hear from you. **JOHN.**

6

● I'M A RESPECTABLE BUT LONELY WIDOW, 60 YEARS OLD. I'm looking for someone to share my life. I like to travel and I'm always willing to learn new things. Please write to **ETHEL.**

7

● WANTED: A STRONG, RELIABLE MAN WITH A GOOD JOB AND LOTS OF MONEY. I'm a slim and pretty 25-year-old nurse with dark hair and brown eyes. If you're young and well-off, call **JAYNE** for an interesting and affectionate companion.

Vocabulary file: Describing people

Complete the table with all the words and phrases in the advertisements for describing people.

appearance	character	lifestyle

2 What questions will the advertisers ask anyone who phones them?

a Work with a partner. Choose one or two of the advertisers and make a list of questions for each person.

b Read out your questions. Can other students guess which advertiser is asking them?

c Using your questions, roleplay the phone conversations with your partner.

Language focus: *have/have got*

a Look at these two sentences from the advertisements.

I have my own house.
I've got two children.

b With *have* and *have got*, how do we form
● negatives?
● questions?
● short answers?

c When do we use *have* and *have got*? What are the differences between them?

➤ Check the rules for *have/have got* in **Grammar Reference 2.3**.

d Work with a partner. Ask and answer about the list below. Find out more information. (Your answers needn't be honest!)

EXAMPLE

A *Have you got a computer?*
B *Yes, I have.*
A *What kind is it?*
B *It's an Apple Mac.*

A *Do you have a computer?*
B *Yes, I do.*
A *What kind is it?*
B *It's an Apple Mac.*

a computer	a boyfriend/girlfriend	a swimming-pool
a pet	a mobile phone	a house or a flat
a bike	an interesting job	any children
a car	any brothers or sisters	a fax machine

e With a new partner, ask and answer about your previous partners.

EXAMPLE

Has Maria got a computer?
Does Maria have a computer?

Yes, she has. It's a …
Yes, she does. It's a …

3 Write your own advert.

a First look at the language that is used in the adverts for describing
● yourself.
● the kind of partner you are looking for.

b Write an advert for yourself or someone else.

Listening and speaking
Making arrangements

1 🔲 *2.3* **Two people are trying to arrange a meeting. Listen and answer these questions.**
  1 Who are the two people?
  2 What tense do they use for talking about their arrangements?

2 **Look at the two diary pages.**

a Can you see any mistakes in the diary notes?

b 🔲 *2.3* Listen again and correct the diaries.

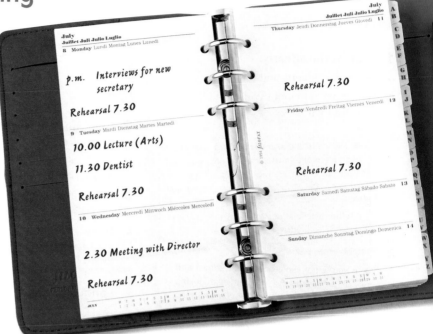

Language focus

1 Time prepositions *in*, *on*, *at*

a Complete these expressions with the correct preposition.

  _____ 10.00   _____ the afternoon
  _____ midday   _____ Thursday morning
  _____ Tuesday   _____ 2.30
  _____ night   _____ the morning

b Look at tapescript 2.3 and check your answers.

c Complete the rules.

> We use _____ with times.
>
> We use _____ with parts of the day.
>
> We use _____ with days.

2 The present continuous with future meaning

a We use the present continuous tense to talk about arrangements in the future. How do we know it means the future?

  EXAMPLES
  Are you doing anything on Tuesday?
  I'm playing tennis at 7.00.

b Look at the completed diaries. Say what each person is doing this week.

  EXAMPLE
  Alan's meeting some people from Poland on Monday morning.

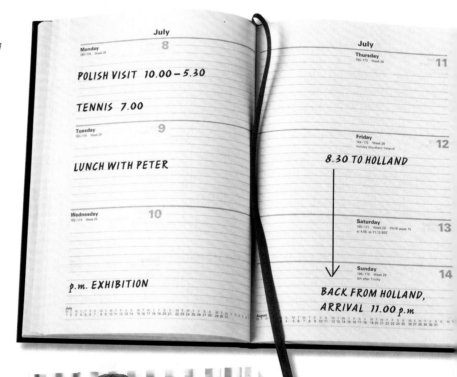

Alan

Mary

Conversation pieces: Making arrangements

Look at these expressions.

a Which of them can you find in tapescript 2.3?

Are you free …?
Are you doing anything …?
Can we …?
Would you like to …?
What about …?
How about …?
Is … any good for you?

Yes, … is fine for me.
Yes, … is OK with me.

No, I can't make …
No, I'm afraid not.
No, I'm sorry. … is no good for me.

b Work with a partner. Try to arrange to meet. Use the expressions above and these times.

Sunday 11.00	Tuesday
the afternoon	this evening
Saturday evening	tomorrow
half past ten	

EXAMPLE
A *Are you free on Sunday?*
B *No, I'm sorry. Sunday is no good for me. What about Monday?*
A *Yes, Monday's fine for me.*

3 Make your own diary page.

a Fill your diary with some arrangements for next week. Leave two half-days clear.

b Work in a group of four. Try to find a time for a meeting.

Pronunciation
Consonants; intonation

1 Voiced and voiceless consonants

Some consonants are voiced and some are voiceless. When you say a voiced consonant, there is a vibration in your throat. When you say a voiceless consonant, there is no vibration. The voiced/voiceless difference can often show two different words.

a Put your fingers on your throat and say these sounds. Write *voiced* and *voiceless* next to the correct list.

/b/ /d/ /g/ /v/ /z/ /l/ /r/ /m/ /n/ /w/ _____

/p/ /t/ /k/ /f/ /s/ /h/ /ʃ/ /tʃ/ _____

b 🔊 *2.4* Listen and tick (✓) the words that you hear.

girl	curl	Sue	zoo
pig	big	pick	pig
pull	bull	rabbit	rapid
two	do	sent	send
come	gum	loose	lose

2 Question intonation

As a general rule intonation rises on a Yes/No question and falls on a statement.

Do you get up early?   *Yes, I do.*

a 🔊 *2.5* Listen. Is it a statement or a question? Tick *S* or *Q* in the table.

	1	2	3	4	5	6	7	8
S								
Q								

b 🔊 *2.6* Listen to the sentences and check your answers.

c 🔊 *2.6* Listen again and repeat.

d 🔊 *2.7* Intonation only rises on Yes/No questions. In *Wh*-questions, the intonation falls. Listen to these examples.

Do you live near here?   *Where do you live?*

e Mark the intonation curve above each question.

1 What's your name?

2 Have you got a pen?

3 What do you do?

4 What are you doing?

5 Do you enjoy it?

6 Are you going out tonight?

f 🔊 *2.8* Listen, check and repeat.

g Work with a partner. Ask and answer the questions.

Extension: Listening and speaking
Talking about your family

1 **Look at this photo of Gloria and her family.**

a Discuss these questions.
1 What is happening in the photo?
2 Who do you think the people are?
3 What relation do you think they are to Gloria?

b 🔊 *2.9* Listen to Gloria talking about the photo and check your ideas. Here are the names she mentions:

Daniel	Oliver	father	Alison	mother
Aaron	Marion	Ben	Rebecca	Josh

c What can you remember about each person?

d One person mentioned isn't in the photo. Who is it?

1 2 3 4 5

6 *Gloria* 7 8 9 10

Vocabulary file: Families

Look at these words and expressions for talking about a family. Check that you understand the meanings.

a Complete the marital status list.

b Complete the list of family relationships.

c Can you add any more family words or expressions?

Marital status:	Family relationships:		More family expressions:
s_____	husband	_wife_	the oldest/youngest
engaged (to)	_____	mother	an older sister
m_____ (to)	son	_____	a little boy/girl
d_____ (from)	_____	sister	parents
separated	uncle	_____	to be expecting a baby
a widow(er)	_____	niece	to be having a baby
	grandfather	_____	to have children
	fiancé	_____	a christening
			grown up

2 Work with a partner. Tell your partner about your family, using family photos, if possible.

3 Write a short description of your family.

a First read Gloria's description of her family.

My family

My father works for a chemical firm. He's a salesman and my mother is a teacher.

I've got one sister and one brother. I'm the second child in the family.

My sister, Marion, is the oldest. She's married and her husband's name is Aaron. They've got three children - two boys and a girl.

My brother Daniel is still studying at university. He's single at the moment, but he's engaged. His fiancée's name is Alison.

I got married last year to Oliver. We don't have any children yet, but we're planning to have three!

b Write about your family, giving information about
- your parents.
- your brothers and sisters (if any) and your position in the family.
- your marital status.
- your partner (if any).
- your children (if any).

3 Life stories

Grammar
The past simple tense

Grammar in use

1 Look at this information.

> In England you can get married when you are 16, but you need your parents' permission until you are 18. In Scotland, however, you can get married at 16 without this. So young English people who want to get married without their parents' permission often run away (elope) to Scotland. The traditional place for these weddings is Gretna Green, a village just over the Scottish border.

a Compare it to your own country.

b What do you think is the right age to get married?

2 Read the newspaper article.

a Answer these questions.
  1 Who are the people in the pictures?
  2 What did the two young people do?
  3 How did the girl's mother feel about this?
  4 What did she do?
  5 What happened in the end?

b Discuss these questions.
  1 What do you think about the people's behaviour?
  2 Who do you think is to blame?

Gretna scene

By PHILIP HARGRAVES

EVEN for Gretna Green, this was a strange story. Marcus Lee-Curtis, 21, and Marie Schearer, 16, weren't runaways. The bridegroom's mother was at the wedding and so were twenty other guests. But the bride's parents weren't there. In fact, they didn't know anything about the wedding until the following week, and then Mrs Schearer was so angry that she attacked Marcus' mother.

Marie first met Marcus when she was only 13. They fell in love and when Marie was 16, she left home and lived with Marcus at his grandmother's house. They

Angry: Christine Schearer

decided to get married. But Marie was only 16 and her parents didn't approve, so they went to Gretna Green.

A week later, Marie's mother opened the local newspaper and saw a photograph of the bride and groom. She wasn't happy and she blamed Marcus' mother. She waited outside the Lee-Curtis' house, and

when Mrs Lee-Curtis came out, Mrs Schearer stopped her. She shouted at her and pulled her hair. When Marcus tried to help his mother, Mrs Schearer hit him in the stomach. Then she drove her car at Mrs Lee-

Curtis and pushed her into a garden. In court today Mrs Schearer apologized. When they came out of court, Marie smiled and said: 'I hope that in time we can all get together.'

Bride Marie, 16, with husband Marcus, 21. 'I hope we can all get together,' she said.

Rules

1 Find examples of the past tense of the verb *to be* (positive and negative) in the text.

2 How do we form the past simple tense of regular verbs?

a Underline examples of regular verbs in the text.

b What do you notice about the spelling of these verbs in the past simple tense?

  smile   stop   try

➤ See p29 for the pronunciation of *-ed* endings.

3 Many common verbs are irregular and don't follow the *-ed* rule.

a List all the irregular verbs in the text.

b Write the infinitive for each verb.

  EXAMPLES
  meet   met   fall   fell

4 Complete these two sentences from the text.

  In fact, they _____ anything about the wedding until the following week.
  But Marie was only 16 and her parents _____ .

- How do we make the negative form of the past simple tense?
- What part of the verb follows *didn't*?
- Is it the same for regular and irregular verbs?

5 Look at these questions from an interview with Marie Schearer.

  Were Marcus' parents at the wedding?
  Why was your mother angry?
  When did you meet Marcus?
  Did you live together?

a How do we make past simple questions with *to be*?

b How do we make questions with other verbs?

➤ Check the rules for the past simple tense in **Grammar Reference 3.1**.

Practice

1 Complete these sentences with the past simple of the verbs in brackets.

  1 Marcus' mother and grandmother _____(be) at the wedding, but Marie's parents _____(not know) anything about it.
  2 Mrs Schearer _____(be) furious when she _____(see) the wedding photo in a newspaper.
  3 She _____(write) to the newspaper and _____ (complain) about the photo.
  4 Mrs Schearer _____(not speak) to her daughter when they _____(appear) in court.
  5 Marie _____(say) that she _____(not be) angry with her mother, because she _____ (understand) how her mother _____(feel).

2 After the trial, a reporter asked Mrs Schearer some questions.

a Write the questions, using this information.
  1 When/ Marie/ meet/ Marcus
  2 When/ she/ leave/ home
  3 Where/ the wedding
  4 Why/ you/ not there
  5 How/ you/ find out/ about it
  6 How/ you/ feel
  7 What/ you/ do
  8 Anyone/ try/ to stop you

b What do you think Mrs Schearer's answers were?

c 🔲 *3.1* Listen and check.

3 Here is another strange romance story from a newspaper.

a Write the story, using this information.

b What do you think about the people?

Stewart McKay/ fall in love with/ Jane
get married/ but there/ be/ problem
both/ have a dog/ and/ dogs/ hate each other
Stewart and Jane/ not want/ get rid of the dogs
decide/ live apart/ while dogs/ alive
live/ 40 miles apart/ three years
not see/ each other very often
life/ be/ very expensive
spend/ a lot of money on phone calls and travel
last week/ Jane's dog/ die
Jane/ go/ to live with Stewart
Jane/ said/ it/ not be/ easy to live apart
I/ not love/ my dog more than Stewart/ but/ I/
  not want/ give her up

c Work with a partner. Write ten questions that a reporter might ask Stewart and Jane.

d Roleplay the interview, using your questions.

4 Choose one of these topics.
- How did your parents meet?
- How did you meet your partner?

a Work in pairs or small groups. Tell your group about your topic, and answer their questions.

b Write about one of the topics.

➤ See **Reflecting on Learning 7**: Verbs p121.

Vocabulary
Money

1 **Look at this list of words associated with money.**

> wealthy   poor   sell   rich   buy
> stock exchange   mean   fortune
> cheap   generous   tax   free   pay
> stocks and shares   bank   cost
> millionaire   price   work   count
> expensive   property   diamonds
> job   jewellery   mortgage   lose

a We can organize the words into a spidergram like this:

inherit   save

Money

spend   earn

sell   buy

price

expensive   cheap

b Complete the legs of the spidergram with words from the list. Some words may go on more than one leg.

2 **Compare your spidergram with the class.**

a Can you add any more words to your spidergram?

b Look at the words again. Choose words that best describe
  • a millionaire's life.
  • your life.

Reading
The Witch of Wall Street

1 **Look at the title of the article and the photograph.**

a What is Wall Street? Where is it?

b What do you think the story is about?

The Witch of

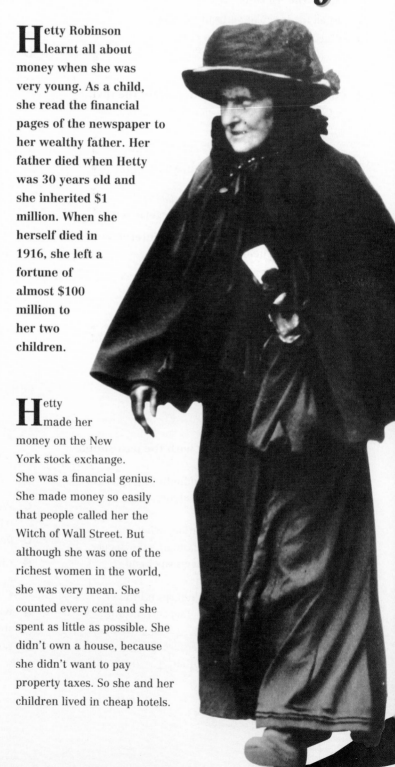

Hetty Robinson learnt all about money when she was very young. As a child, she read the financial pages of the newspaper to her wealthy father. Her father died when Hetty was 30 years old and she inherited $1 million. When she herself died in 1916, she left a fortune of almost $100 million to her two children.

Hetty made her money on the New York stock exchange. She was a financial genius. She made money so easily that people called her the Witch of Wall Street. But although she was one of the richest women in the world, she was very mean. She counted every cent and she spent as little as possible. She didn't own a house, because she didn't want to pay property taxes. So she and her children lived in cheap hotels.

2 Read the article quickly and answer these questions.

1 Who was the Witch of Wall Street?
2 When did she live?
3 Who were Ned and Edward?
4 What was strange about her life?
5 How did she die?

all Street

She spent almost nothing on clothes, and wore the same long black dress every day. She washed it herself, but to save soap she only washed the bottom of the dress, where it touched the ground. Other people had their own offices, but Hetty used a desk in the bank where she kept her money, because it didn't cost anything. She sat in the bank and ate her sandwiches while she bought and sold stocks and shares. If the bank complained, she just moved all her money to another bank.

Hetty's family paid the price for her meanness. When she was 33 she married a millionaire, Edward Green and they had two children. Green, however, lost all his money, so Hetty left him. When her son, Ned, injured his knee, Hetty didn't want to pay for a doctor, so she took him to a free hospital for poor people. Unfortunately the doctor knew that Hetty was rich and he asked for money. Hetty refused and took the boy away. His leg didn't get better and two years later doctors removed it.

But eventually Ned got his revenge. At the age of 81 Hetty had an argument with a shop assistant about the price of a bottle of milk. She became so angry that she had a stroke and died. So Hetty's meanness finally killed her. Ned inherited half his mother's fortune, and he spent it all on parties, holidays and expensive jewellery. He even bought a chamber pot covered with diamonds!

3 Read the article again. Mark these sentences *True* (✓) or *False* (✗). Correct the false sentences.

EXAMPLE
She came from a poor family.
She didn't come from a poor family. Her parents were wealthy.

1 She knew a lot about finance when she was young. ☐
2 She owned a big house. ☐
3 She didn't have many clothes. ☐
4 She sent her clothes to a laundry. ☐
5 She rented an office in Wall Street. ☐
6 She had lunch in restaurants. ☐
7 She married a rich man. ☐
8 She sent her son to the best hospital in New York. ☐
9 She died in an accident. ☐
10 Her son invested her money. ☐

4 Discuss these questions.
1 Give three reasons why Hetty was called the Witch of Wall Street.
2 What do you think is
   • the worst example of Hetty's meanness?
   • the funniest example of her meanness?
   • the most interesting part of the story?
   • the most ironic part of her life?
3 Why do you think Hetty was so mean?
4 Do you know any other examples of mean behaviour?

Language focus: *so … that …*

a Look at these two sentences:

Hetty became angry.   She had a stroke.

The second sentence is the result of the first sentence. We can show it like this:

*Hetty became **so** angry **that** she had a stroke.*

b Join these sentences in the same way.
1 Hetty was mean. She refused to pay for a doctor.
2 Ned's injury was bad. He lost his leg.
3 Hetty was rich. She could buy anything.
4 She was clever. She made millions of dollars.
5 Hetty made money easily. People called her the Witch of Wall Street.

---

5 Look at this newspaper headline.

THE KINDEST MAN IN THE WORLD DIES

a Work in groups and discuss ideas for the story.
b Write the story, using this format:
   • The basic details of his life
   • Examples of his kindness
   • How he died

Listening and speaking
Telling your life story

1 Geoff is telling Sally about his life.

a   ▣ 3.2 Listen. In column A, number the places where Geoff lived in the correct order.

b   Match the photographs to the places in column A.

c   Match the places in column A to an item in columns B and C.

d   ▣ 3.2 Listen again and check.

A Where?	B How long?	C Reason for leaving
☐ Scotland	nearly five years	grandfather died
☐ Manchester	six months	grandfather was ill
☐ Singapore	two years	
☐ London	not very long	Geoff went to university
☑ Peru	four years	father's company closed down
☐ Canada	eight years	too cold

Geoff, Bonnie and a llama!

2 Discuss these questions.

  1 Where does the conversation take place?

  2 Why does Geoff say: 'It's difficult to say.'?

  3 What positive and negative effects do you think this had on his life?

  4 What do you think of Geoff's life? Does it sound interesting/boring/difficult?

3 Write a summary of Geoff's life, using the table in **1**.

Conversation pieces: Life events
Look at these expressions.

I was born in …
I grew up in …
I started school in …
I left school in …
I went to university/college.
I started work in …
I got a job in …

I lost my job.
I was unemployed.
The factory/farm closed down.
We moved to …
We stayed/lived there for …
I got married/divorced.
My grandfather died.

The far north, beautiful but cold!

4 Talk about your life.

a   Make a list of key events in your life with times and places.

b   Work with a partner. Tell your partner your life story, using the expressions above. Answer any questions that your partner asks.

5 Write your life story.

Captain Geoff in the tropics

The CN Tower

At Gran's house

Geoff and cousin, in Hyde Park

Pronunciation
-ed ending; word stress

1 The past simple *-ed* ending

The regular past simple *-ed* ending can be
pronounced in three different ways, /t/, /d/ and /ɪd/.

a Match the endings to the correct type of verb.
 1 When the verb ends with a voiced consonant
  e.g. *rob – robbed, use – used.*
 2 When the verb ends with a voiceless consonant
  e.g. *walk – walked, laugh – laughed.*
 3 When the verb ends with /t/ or /d/
  e.g. *want – wanted, need – needed.*

b Complete the table with these verbs.

attacked	blamed	promised	waited
liked	decided	helped	pushed
counted	started	watched	lived
avoided	talked	seemed	turned

/d/	/t/	/ɪd/

c 🔲 *3.3* Listen, check and repeat.

2 Word stress with two syllables

In words with more than one syllable we usually
stress only one of the syllables.

EXAMPLES

• •
problem

 • •
expect

a Say these words. Which syllable has the stress?
Mark the syllable with the stress.

study	question	attack	picture
money	machine	headache	spelling
woman	tennis	number	extra
pronounce	again	people	address
children	sorry	colour	divorced
model	forget	repeat	husband

b 🔲 *3.4* Listen, check and repeat.

c Which syllable usually has the stress?

Extension: Reading and listening
Shark attack!

1 **The illustration shows a scene from a true story.**

a What do you think happened?

b What other words do you expect to find in the article? Make a list.

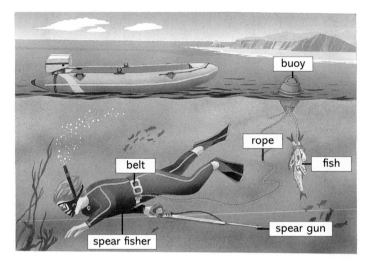

2 **The paragraphs of the magazine article are in the wrong order.**

a Number the paragraphs in the correct order.

b How did you decide on the order? What clues did you use?

c 🔊 *3.5* Listen and check your order.

d Which words in your list did you find in the text?

Language focus: Adverbs and adjectives

a Complete the example sentences from the text.

Adverbs describe a verb.

EXAMPLE
Fox floated _____ to the surface.

Adjectives describe a noun.

EXAMPLE
He saw a _____ fish.

b Find these words in the text. Are they adverbs or adjectives?

c Which verb or noun does each word describe?

well	long	suddenly	huge
quickly	fast	hard	small
carefully	desperately	big	great
dangerous	large	annual	safe

➤ Check the rules for adverbs and adjectives in **Grammar Reference 3.2.**

---

3 **What do you think Rodney Fox did after the attack?**

a Look at this list of ideas. What other possibilities can you think of?
- He started a campaign to stop spear-fishing.
- He became a doctor.
- He started to study sharks.
- He gave up spear-fishing.
- He hunted the shark that attacked him.
- He tried to kill as many sharks as possible.
- He started a campaign to protect the great white shark.
- He never went in the sea again.

b Work with a partner and make your choice. More than one may be correct. Discuss your choices with the class.

c 🔊 *3.6* Listen to the rest of the story and check your ideas.

d Discuss these questions.
1 What did Rodney Fox do and why?
2 What do you think of Rodney Fox's reaction?

4 **Write the final paragraph to complete the story of Rodney Fox.**

➤ See **Reflecting on Learning 8**: Correction p121.

SHARK ATTACK!

☐ He thought that this was the end. He fought desperately, but the big shark pulled him down and down. Then suddenly the rope broke and Fox floated slowly to the surface. 'Shark! Shark!' he called.

☐ Quickly he pushed his fingers into the shark's eyes. The shark opened its mouth and Fox escaped, swimming as fast as possible to the surface. He thought he was safe, but when he looked down he saw the shark's huge mouth just below him again.

☐ Near the end of the day, he looked down and saw a large fish on the sand below him. He dived down to get it. Suddenly something hit him. It knocked the spear gun from his hand and pushed him through the water. He looked round and saw that he was in the mouth of a shark. It was a great white shark, one of the largest and most dangerous sharks in the world.

☐ Other spear-fishers heard him and hurried to help him. They lifted him carefully into a boat and took him to the beach. The nearest hospital was 60 kilometres away and during the long journey one of the spear-fishers held Fox's insides in place. At the hospital he needed 462 stitches, but he survived.

☐ So he kicked the shark's nose hard and it turned away. But then it attacked the fish on the buoy. It swallowed the buoy and the fish. It dived down and the rope on his belt pulled Fox under the water again.

1 It was 1963 and Rodney Fox was in the sea off the coast of South Australia. It was the annual spear-fishing championship. Fox did well that day. He caught a lot of fish and he tied them to a small buoy. There was a rope from the buoy to his belt.

4 The future

Grammar

will; first conditional

Grammar in use

1 Look at the title of the article. What is it about?

2 Read the text and tick (✓) what the prizewinners will do.

- ☐ see a show at a West End theatre
- ☐ go to the hotel in a taxi
- ☐ have dinner at the Savoy Hotel
- ☐ go to Buckingham Palace
- ☐ arrive in London
- ☐ meet the stars of the show
- ☐ travel in a limousine
- ☐ visit a casino
- ☐ have dinner with the stars of the show
- ☐ dance at a nightclub
- ☐ go back to the hotel after the show
- ☐ stay at the Ritz Hotel

TRAVEL MONTHLY

Enter our free competition and win a night to remember in ...

LONDON!

If you are our lucky winner, you'll have the best night of your life in our exciting capital city. Your night to remember will start when you arrive in London. If you arrive by train or bus, our representative will meet you at the station.

West End Shows

Adelphi Theatre
'Sunset Boulevard'

Apollo Victoria
'Starlight Express'

Cambridge Theatre
'Fame – The Musical'

Drury Lane Theatre
'Miss Saigon'

Palace Theatre
'Les Misérables'

New London Theatre
'Cats'

Where will you stay?
Our limousine will take you to the world famous Savoy Hotel. You'll have some time to relax before dinner if you're tired after the journey. Dinner will be a five-course meal with champagne in the hotel.

What will you do?
Then our limousine will take you to the theatre to see a West End show. You'll have the best seats in the house and after the show you'll go backstage to meet the stars. And that won't be the end of your night to remember. From the theatre you'll go to a top London nightclub, where you'll dance the night away!

Rules

1 Look at the text again.

a Find these forms of the future with *will*:
- a positive statement (a long and a short form)
- a negative statement
- a question

b How do we make these forms?

c When do we use *will* for the future? Compare *will* to the use of the present continuous with future meaning.

2 We use *will* in first conditionals.

a Complete these sentences from the text.

If you _____ our lucky winner, you _____ the best night of your life in our exciting capital city.

You _____ some time to relax before dinner if you _____ tired after the journey.

b Complete the rule:

> In first conditionals we use the _____ tense in the *if* clause and _____ in the main clause.

c Do the sentences talk about the past, present, or the future? What does the first conditional describe?

➤ Check the rules for *will* and the first conditional in **Grammar References 4.1** and **4.2**.

Menu

Cream of Tomato Soup with Gin and Croutons
Lobster with Garlic Dressing
Lentil Salad with Roasted Peppers and Feta Cheese

****

Roast Duck with Mushrooms and Bacon
Salmon with Tomato and Lemon Vinaigrette
Pork with Apple Slices, Calvados and Cream

****

Apple and Almond Tart with Cream
Dark Chocolate Tart
Fresh Fruit Salad

****

Cheese and biscuits

****

Coffee and Chocolates

Practice

1 Look at your answers for Grammar in use 2 again. Work with a partner and say what the prizewinners will do and what they won't do.

EXAMPLES
They'll see a show at a West End Theatre.
They won't go to the hotel in a taxi.

2 If you win the competition, what will you do?

a Make questions using this information and *will*.

EXAMPLE
How will you get to London?

1 How/ get to London	**6** Which theatre/ go to
2 anyone/ meet you	**7** Which show/ see
3 Where/ stay	**8** have/ good seats
4 What/ have/ for dinner	**9** meet/ anyone famous
5 How/ get to the theatre	**10** What/ do/ after the show

b Work with a partner. Look at the competition information again and ask and answer the questions.

3 Here is some more information about the competition.

a Match a clause in A and a clause in B. Make complete sentences using the first conditional.

EXAMPLES
*If you arrive by train, our representative **will** meet you at the station.*
*We'll collect you from your home **if you** live in London.*

A	B
arrive by train	have time to go to the shops on Saturday
collect you from your home	not want to go to a nightclub
have some time to relax	tired after the journey
enjoy the show	arrange a nanny to look after them
want to meet the stars of the show	really enjoy the nightclub
our limousine/ take you for a city tour	take you backstage
take you back to the hotel	live in London
like dancing	give you two free tickets for your friends
have children	want to see London by night
want to do some shopping	our representative/ meet you at the station

b 🔲 *4.1* Listen and check.

4 What do you want to know about the future?

a Write five questions with *will*.

b Work with a partner. Ask your questions. Your partner will make predictions for you.

5 Write a competition article.

a Work in groups. Think of a new prize for a competition. Here are some ideas:
- a weekend in Paris
- a flight in a hot air balloon
- a day at the races
- a visit to a casino

b Write an article to describe your prize.

Vocabulary
Country adjectives

1 **We use country adjectives to show nationality and language.**

EXAMPLES

They are from Japan.
*They are **Japanese**.*
*They speak **Japanese**.*

a There are several ways of forming country adjectives. Look at this table.

-an	-ish	-ese	-i	irregular
America – *American*	England – *English*	Japan – *Japanese*	Iraq – *Iraqi*	France – *French*
Hungary – *Hungarian*				

b Complete the table with the countries from the box below. You can use a dictionary to help you find the adjectives.

Germany	Italy	Turkey	the Netherlands
Israel	Argentina	Thailand	Scotland
Ireland	Belgium	Morocco	Pakistan
Russia	Norway	Greece	Egypt Poland
Portugal	Austria	Denmark	Brazil
China	Mexico	Korea	Spain

c 🔲 *4.2* Listen and check your ideas.

d Add your own country if it isn't mentioned.

2 **The names of countries have different stress patterns.**

EXAMPLES

● ·   · ●   · · ● ·
Egypt   Japan   Argentina

The stress pattern sometimes changes in the adjective.

EXAMPLES

● · ·   · ● ·
Italy   Italian

a Mark the syllable with the stress on each word in the table.

b 🔲 *4.2* Listen again and check your answers.

c Look at the adjectives in the table and answer these questions.
  1 Which are languages?
  2 Which languages are spoken in the other countries?

➤ See **Reflecting on Learning 9**: Dealing with unknown words p121.

Reading
The end of the melting pot?

1 **Immigration is a political issue in some parts of the world.**

a Discuss these questions.
  1 Why do people go to live in another country?
  2 What benefits can immigrants bring to a country?
  3 What problems can large-scale immigration cause?
  4 Should immigrants conform to the local culture?
  5 What should governments do about immigration?

b Look quickly at the text. Choose the correct answers to these questions, according to the article.

  1 What is the article about?
  ☐ America's population is getting too large.
  ☐ African Americans will soon be in the majority in the USA.
  ☐ The USA is changing because of immigration.

  2 Why are today's immigrants different from earlier immigrants?
  ☐ They integrate easily into American culture.
  ☐ They come to the USA for jobs.
  ☐ They keep their own language and culture.

  3 Why are African Americans very worried about the situation?
  ☐ The immigrants compete with them for jobs and houses.
  ☐ The immigrants don't speak English.
  ☐ The immigrants become politicians and lawyers.

2 **Read the text again and find**
  ● all the racial groups mentioned.
  ● reasons why people are concerned about the situation.

3 **Mark these sentences *True (✓), False (✗)* or *Don't Know (?)*.**

  1 America's population will be 383 million by the year 2050. ☐
  2 Hispanics make up 10 per cent of the population at the moment. ☐
  3 African Americans are currently the largest racial minority in the USA. ☐
  4 Today's immigrants try to integrate into American culture. ☐
  5 The number of people who don't speak English is increasing. ☐
  6 Robert Byrd wants stricter immigration controls. ☐
  7 Illegal immigrants only compete for jobs. ☐
  8 Illegal immigrants can't find jobs in the USA. ☐

4 Complete these sentences with the verbs in brackets.

1 If immigration _____ (rise), Hispanics _____ (overtake) African Americans.

2 If you _____ (go) into the supermarket in Rockville, you _____ (not hear) any English.

3 Schools _____ (teach) in immigrant languages if parents _____ (get) their demands.

4 If more immigrants _____ (come), there _____ (be) fewer jobs for African Americans.

5 The middle classes _____ (lose) their cheap servants if immigration _____ (stop).

5 Discuss these questions, giving reasons for your answers.

1 Why do you think the new immigrants don't integrate as earlier immigrants did?

2 Do you think they will integrate in the future?

3 What is the implication of Senator Byrd's expression 'these people'?

4 According to the article, what is the basic cause of the immigration problem in the USA?

5 What do you think the writer feels about the situation in the article?

6 How do you feel about the situation described in the article?

7 What results do you think that the language issue will have?

The end of the melting pot?

If present levels of immigration continue, by the year 2050 America's population will increase by 50 per cent to 383 million.

More importantly the racial balance will change. Hispanics will overtake Blacks (or African Americans, as they are now called) to become the largest minority at 21 per cent. Asians and Pacific Islanders will increase five times to more than 12 per cent. This will push the total of minorities to over 50 per cent of the population.

The USA is a country of immigrants, but today's newcomers are different. Immigrants in the nineteenth and early twentieth centuries became part of the great American melting pot. They learnt the language and integrated into the culture of their new home. But today's immigrants keep their own culture. They have their own TV channels, daily newspapers and magazines.

The English language has almost disappeared in many places. Parts of Florida, California and Texas are now Spanish-speaking. The Hispanic community is a billion dollar market and companies produce adverts in Spanish. In a huge supermarket in Rockville, Maryland, every customer is from the Far East. You'll hear Japanese, Korean and Chinese, but

The Statue of Liberty: still the entrance to the New World?

you won't hear any English. And this language problem won't get any better. Immigrant parents are demanding education for their children in their own language. If this happens, it will soon be possible to grow up in America and never speak English.

Politicians are asking: How far will this go? What kind of country will it produce? Senator Robert Byrd, a Democrat from West Virginia recently told the Senate: 'When I phone the local garage I can't understand the person on the other end of the line and he can't understand me. These people are all over the place and they don't speak English. Do we want more of this?' Both Democrats and Republicans are demanding strict immigration controls.

The biggest problem is illegal immigration. African Americans are very worried about this, because the illegal immigrants compete with them for houses, schools and especially jobs. Work is the key to the problem. While the white middle classes complain, many of them (including politicians and lawyers) employ illegal immigrants as cheap nannies, housekeepers, gardeners, chauffeurs and maids. And if there are jobs, the immigrants will continue to come. ■

Listening and speaking
Messages

1 **You will hear the messages on Jack Waterman's office answerphone.**

a  *4.3* Listen and match the people and messages.

Teresa	going to the States
son	return call
Peter	no message
wife	long meeting
Dennis	party
Sarah Jones	traffic jam on the M25
mother	results of the Dutch project

b Answer these questions.
1 Where is Mrs Waterman?
2 When will she phone her husband?
3 When does Sarah Jones think she will arrive?
4 Why does she leave a telephone number?
5 Where will Dennis be this afternoon?
6 What doesn't Jack's mother like?
7 What does Teresa want to talk about?
8 How long will she be away?
9 What does Jack's son want?

c  *4.3* Listen again and check.

Conversation pieces: Leaving messages

a Complete the answerphone message.

❝ *Hello, Waterman International. Mr Waterman's office. I'm _____ there's nobody in the _____ at the moment, but if you _____ your name and _____ , Mr Waterman will _____ back to you as soon as possible. Please _____ after the tone. Thank you.* ❞

b Complete the expressions with these verbs.

ring	put	drop	return	give
get	call	be	phone	have

I'll _____ back to you.
I'm _____ about the results.
I'll _____ them in the post.
I'll _____ you a ring.
... in case you want to _____ me back.
I'm just _____ your call.
I'll _____ a chat with them.
I'll _____ you a line.
I'll _____ in touch.
I'm just _____ to say ...

c  *4.3* Listen again and check your answers.

Language focus:
will for spontaneous decisions

We also use *will* when we make decisions as we are speaking.

a Look at these sentences from the answerphone messages.

*Anyway, **I'll give** you a call this evening.*
*As you're not there, **I'll have** a chat with the agency.*

b Look at tapescript 4.3 and underline more examples with *will* for a spontaneous decision.

2 Practise giving and leaving messages.

a Work with a partner. Take it in turns to be the secretary speaking to Mr Waterman.
Use the information and expressions on p36 and give Mr Waterman the messages.

EXAMPLES

There were some messages while you were out.
Peter has got the results of the Dutch project. He'll put them in the post.
Your wife won't be back till tomorrow. Her meeting …

b Take it in turns to be the caller and the secretary. Use these situations to leave messages.

Caller Phone Mr Waterman and leave a message with the secretary.

Secretary Write down the message. Check it back with the caller.

1 You're going to be in London for four days. You're staying at the Great Western Hotel, Paddington. You want to meet Mr Waterman.

2 You've got a meeting with Mr Waterman at three o'clock this afternoon, but you don't feel well.

3 You are Mr Waterman's son. While you were at your friend's house, someone stole the car.

4 Mr Waterman phoned you yesterday for some information. You haven't got it yet, but you think it will arrive tomorrow.

5 You had an interesting meeting this morning. You have some confidential information, but you don't want to give it over the phone.

6 You're having dinner with Mr Waterman this evening. You're phoning to make the arrangements. Tell him when and where you will meet.

c Think of two more messages to leave with the secretary.

3 Use a tape recorder, at home or at school, to practise leaving messages on an answerphone.

Pronunciation
/ɪ/, /iː/; sentence stress

1 The sounds /ɪ/ and /iː/

Some vowels are short, e.g. /ɒ/ (as in *dog*).
Some vowels are long, e.g. /ɔː/ (as in *door*).
The short/long difference is important, because it can show two different words.

EXAMPLES

cat /æ/   *cart* /ɑː/
fit /ɪ/   *feet* /iː/

In this unit you will practise one of these short/long differences: /ɪ/ and /iː/. You will practise others in later units.

a Say these words.

hill	he'll	it	eat
live	leave	slip	sleep
will	we'll	his	he's
chip	cheap	rich	reach
sit	seat	hit	heat
fill	feel	this	these

b 🔊 *4.4* Listen and tick (✔) the words you hear.

c 🔊 *4.5* Listen again and repeat.

2 Sentence stress

We saw in Unit 3 that not all the syllables in a word are stressed equally. This is the same for sentences. Not all of the syllables are stressed equally.

a 🔊 *4.6* Listen to these sentences. What kind of words have the stress?

I 'll see you tomorrow.

What do you want?

I 'm going to have a drink.

b 🔊 *4.7* Each sentence in the conversation has two stressed syllables. Listen and mark them.

A Where are you going?

B I'm going to the shops.

A Can I come with you?

B Yes, if you like.

A Are you taking the car?

B I want to walk.

A But it's starting to rain.

B That doesn't matter.

A Oh, I'll stay at home then.

B OK. See you later.

c 🔊 *4.7* Listen and check.

d 🔊 *4.7* Listen again and repeat.

Reading
Eye to eye

1 What do you know about eyes?

a Discuss these questions.
1 Why are brown eyes more common in hotter parts of the world?
2 Why does our eyesight get worse as we get older?
3 Why are our eyes so important to us?
4 How do someone's eyes show whether they like something?
5 Why do people wear make-up?
6 People normally don't look at each other in lifts. Why not?

b Now read the text and compare your ideas.

2 Each paragraph has a sentence missing.

a Read the missing sentences and write the number of each sentence in the correct place.
1 But when we don't like something, they become smaller.
2 This is why lovers gaze into each other's eyes.
3 Many people believe that blue eyes are more delicate than brown eyes.
4 Pictures in the Pyramids show that the ancient Egyptians – both men and women – used it.
5 The lens focuses the light onto the retina at the back of the eye.

b How did you decide the correct positions?

3 Label the diagram with these words. What is each part of the eye for?

eyelid eyelash pupil iris retina optic nerve

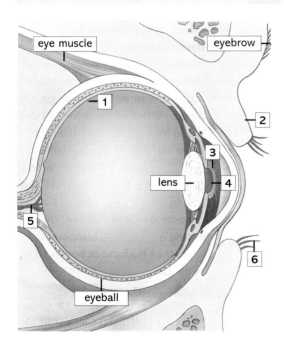

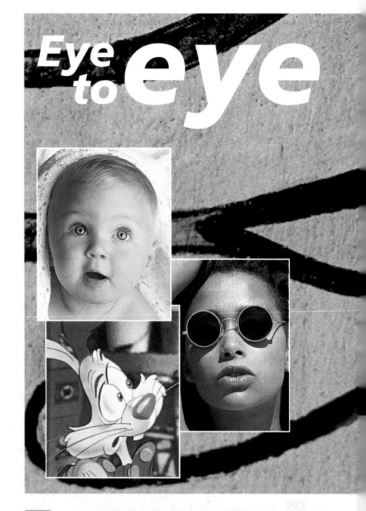

The coloured part of the eye is called the iris. There are three basic eye colours – brown, blue and green. A few albino people have red or pink eyes, but these are very rare. In fact they are just as tough as brown eyes, although they are more sensitive to light.

We only see part of the eyeball, although the whole eye is as big as a table tennis ball. Light enters the eye through the pupil and passes through the lens. The retina sends the signal to the brain along the optic nerve. The image on the retina is actually upside-down, but the brain corrects it. As we get older our eyesight becomes worse. This happens because the lens isn't as flexible as when we are young and the eye muscles are weaker.

Our eyes are the most important of our five senses. We receive 80% of our information about the world through our eyes. We also send signals to other people with our eyes. Some eye signals are unconscious. When we look at something nice, our pupils dilate (get bigger). We cry when we are

unhappy and sometimes when we are very happy. But we can also control some eye signals. For example, we can wink at someone or raise an eyebrow. Sunglasses make someone appear mysterious or dangerous, because they hide the eyes and so we can't see the signals.

We find large eyes more attractive. Children have large eyes in proportion to their heads. Cartoon characters always have large eyes, too. We can't actually change our eyes, but we can make them look bigger with make-up. Eye make-up isn't new. False eyelashes can make eyelashes longer. Eye shadow on the eyelids can make the eyes look bigger and more dramatic. Glasses can also make eyes look bigger.

We do not normally look into someone's eyes for long, especially when they are very close. Eye contact can be very threatening, so people only do it when they want to threaten someone. It is also very intimate. It's also why people don't look at each other in lifts.

4 Look at the text again.

a Find as many examples as possible of
- eye colours.
- eye signals.
- ways of changing the appearance of eyes.

b Can you add any more examples?

5 Discuss these questions.

1 Why do women generally wear eye make-up rather than men?

2 In some cultures people cry in public. In other cultures they don't. What about your culture? When is it acceptable to cry in public?

3 What restrictions are there in your culture on eye contact?

6 A lot of expressions have the word *eye* in them.

a Here are some examples in English. Match them with their meanings.

to see eye to eye with someone	*to ignore something*
to keep an eye on someone or something	*to attract someone's attention*
to catch someone's eye	*to agree with someone*
to look someone (straight) in the eye	*to watch carefully*
to give someone the eye	*to be the favourite*
to be someone's blue-eyed boy/girl	*to show that you are interested in someone*
to turn a blind eye to something	*to be direct with someone*

b Do you have similar expressions in your language?

Language focus: *as … as …*

We can compare things using *as … as …* .

a Look at these sentences.
Blue eyes are as tough as brown eyes.
Green eyes aren't as common as blue or brown eyes.

b Write sentences using this information and *as … as …* .

1 brown eyes/ sensitive to light/ blue eyes

2 in hot countries blue eyes/ common/ brown eyes

3 whole eye/ big/ table tennis ball

4 small eyes/ attractive/ large eyes

5 women's eyebrows/ thick/ men's

6 lens in an old person's eye/ flexible/ a young person's

7 eye make-up/ old/ history

8 our ears/ important/ our eyes

Vocabulary
Clothes

1 **Look at these different kinds of clothes.**

a Match the words to the pictures. Check the meaning of any new words.

> shirt   socks   jumper   skirt
> coat   tie   blouse   cap   bra
> tracksuit   vest   shorts   jacket
> trousers   jeans   shoes   dress
> tights   hat   trainers   T-shirt
> boots   sandals   stockings
> knickers   underpants   swimsuit

b Organize the words into these categories:
Things that you wear
- on your head
- above your waist
- below your waist
- on your feet

Language focus: Clothes with plural names

a Look at these two dialogues. What do you notice about *jeans*?

A *Do you like **this** shirt?*
B *Yes, how much **is it**?*
A *__It's__ £25.*

A *Do you like **these** jeans?*
B *Yes, how much **are they**?*
A *__They're__ £45.*

b The names of some clothes, like *jeans*, are always plural even though there is only one item. Find more examples in the list of clothes.

c Work with a partner. Choose items from the list. Make dialogues like the ones in **a** above.

d To describe a quantity of clothes with plural names, we use the expression *a pair of/pairs of*.

EXAMPLES
a shirt   *three shirts*
a pair of jeans   *two pairs of jeans*
a pair of shoes   *three pairs of shoes*

➤ See **Grammar Reference 5.2**.

2 **Stand back-to-back with a partner and describe what he/she is wearing today.**

3 **You are going to New York for a long weekend. Decide what time of year you are going, what you will pack, and why.**

Listening and speaking
In a clothes shop

1 Look at the conversation.

a What does the woman buy?

b Number the lines in the correct order.

c 📼 **5.4** Listen and check.

☐ Anything else?

☐ Just a minute. No, I'm sorry, we haven't. What about the black one?

☐ |1| Can I help you?

☐ Thank you. That's £7.50 change.

☐ Yes, how much are these T-shirts?

☐ No, it's too dark. I'd prefer something lighter.

☐ That's £12.50 then, please.

☐ Yes, that's nice. I'll take it.

☐ Thank you. Goodbye.

☐ Here you are.

☐ I like this one, but it isn't big enough. Have you got it in a larger size?

☐ They're £12.50 each.

☐ How about this blue one?

☐ No, that's all, thank you.

2 📼 **5.5 Listen to the conversations. What do the five customers buy?**

Language focus: *too/enough*

a Look at these two sentences from the conversation.
*It isn't big **enough**.*   *It's **too** dark.*

b Rewrite the sentences, using the words *small* and *light* and keeping the same meaning.

c Rewrite these sentences to keep the same meaning, using the words in brackets.

1 They're too loose. (*tight*)
2 It isn't long enough. (*short*)
3 They aren't dark enough. (*light*)
4 These are too small. (*large*)
5 You're too short. (*tall*)
6 It's too cold. (*warm*)
7 It isn't thick enough. (*thin*)
8 It's too low. (*high*)

Conversation pieces: Shopping

a Complete these expressions.

Asking about and saying what you want:

Can I _____ you?
I'd like …
I'd prefer …
Could I _____ …?
Have you got any …?
No, thank you. I'm only _____ .
Let me know if you need any

_____ .
(Would you like) _____ else?
Is that all?

Asking about and saying prices:

How _____ | is this/that …?
* | are these/those …?*

It's …
They're … (each).
Have you got anything cheaper?
That's … altogether.

Making a decision:

I'll take …
I'll have …
That's all, thank you.
No, I'll leave it. _____ anyway.

b Decide which expressions the customer says and which expressions the assistant says.

c Look at tapescripts 5.4 and 5.5 and check your answers.

3 Work with a partner and roleplay the conversations, using tapescript 5.5.

4 Work with a partner. Roleplay conversations for these situations in a clothes shop.

1 You don't know what you want yet.
2 You want a black T-shirt in a large size.
3 You want some jeans. You try on a pair but they're too big.
4 You want to buy a jumper and some blue socks.
5 You want to buy some brown shoes. The first ones that you try on aren't right.
6 You want a jacket and a black leather belt.

Pronunciation /ɒ/, /ɔː/; reduced vowels

1 The sounds /ɒ/ and /ɔː/

a Look at these words. Some of them have a short /ɒ/ vowel sound and some have a long /ɔː/ vowel sound.

b Write the words in the correct column.

saw	jog	song	all	got
caught	want	cost		boring
socks	shorts	ball		stop
what	four	sport		bought

/ɒ/	/ɔː/
dog	door

c 🔊 **5.6** Listen and check.

d 🔊 **5.6** Listen again and repeat.

2 Reduced vowels

a In connected speech the vowels in some words are reduced to the sound /ə/.

EXAMPLE
/ə/
What are you doing?

What kinds of words do you think are reduced in this way?

b Look at these sentences. Circle the reduced vowels.

1 How much are these jeans?
2 Does he like this shirt?
3 I need a pair of socks.
4 Could I try them on?
5 Come on. It's time to go.
6 There's a good film on TV.
7 I can play the piano.
8 Were you at home yesterday?
9 No, I was out all day.
10 Here's a postcard from Jane.

c 🔊 **5.7** Listen and check.

d Practise saying the sentences.

➤ See **Reflecting on Learning 10**: Pair and group work p121.

Extension: Listening and speaking
You've got what it takes

1 Look at the song.

a What is it about? What do you think the missing words are?

b 🔊 **5.8** Listen and check your ideas.

c 🔊 **5.8** Listen again and complete the song.

2 In the song, the singer compares a real person to an ideal person.

a What characteristics does that ideal person have? How important are they?

b What characteristics do you think the real person has got? What do you think makes her attractive to the singer?

3 What makes a person attractive to you?

a Work in groups. Here are some characteristics. Add some more.

- a sense of humour
- generous
- broad shoulders
- intelligent
- a good figure
- well-educated
- good-looking
- a good job
- a lot of money

b From your list choose the ten features that are most important to you and then put them in order of importance.

c Compare your order with the class.

4 Write a description of your ideal partner, saying what characteristics are important and why.

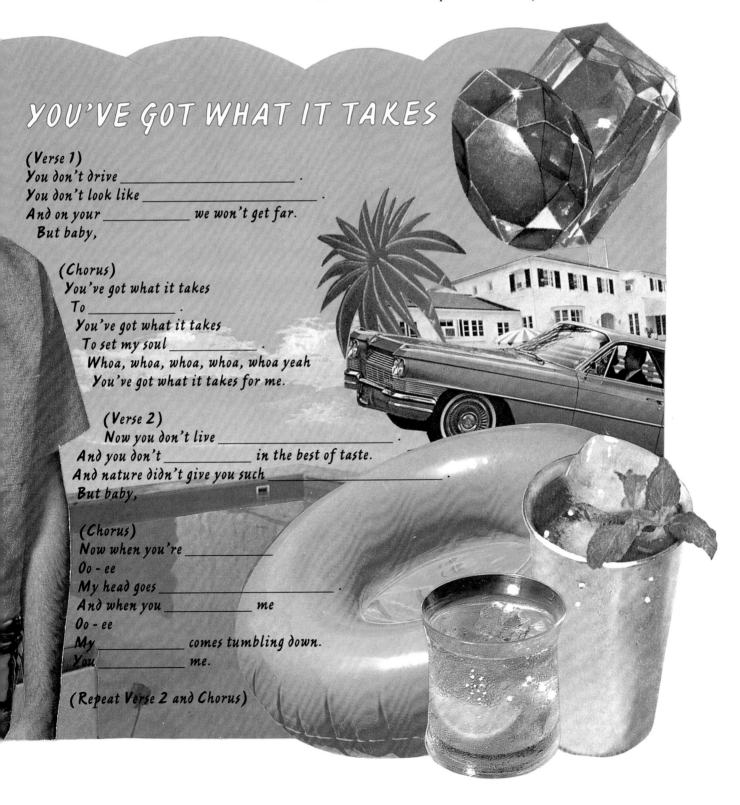

YOU'VE GOT WHAT IT TAKES

(Verse 1)
You don't drive _____ .
You don't look like _____ .
And on your _____ we won't get far.
  But baby,

(Chorus)
  You've got what it takes
  To _____ .
  You've got what it takes
  To set my soul _____ .
  Whoa, whoa, whoa, whoa, whoa yeah
    You've got what it takes for me.

(Verse 2)
  Now you don't live _____ .
And you don't _____ in the best of taste.
And nature didn't give you such _____ .
  But baby,

(Chorus)
Now when you're _____
Oo - ee
My head goes _____ .
And when you _____ me
Oo - ee
My _____ comes tumbling down.
You _____ me.

(Repeat Verse 2 and Chorus)

6 People and places

Grammar
The past continuous tense

Grammar in use

1 **Look at the pictures. What is happening in each one?**

2 **The pictures are in the wrong order.**

a Work with a partner and decide the correct order.

b Read the story and check.

An embarrassing incident

One day last summer I was walking through the local park. It was a hot day and I was eating an ice cream. As I was walking past the boating lake, I saw my friends, Carol and Jim. They were taking their dog for a walk. When we met, we stopped for a chat. While we were talking, the dog suddenly jumped up and tried to get my ice cream. I pulled my hand away and unfortunately the ice cream came out of the cone. Now there was a bald man behind me. The poor man wasn't doing any harm. He was just sitting on a bench and reading a newspaper. Well, when I pulled my hand away, the ice cream flew through the air and it landed on the man's head. I didn't know whether to laugh or cry, but Carol and Jim did. When I looked at them, they weren't just laughing, they were in hysterics. But I was terribly embarrassed.

Rules

1 **Look at the tenses in the story.**

a Complete these sentences.

I _____ an ice cream.
The poor man _____ any harm.
They _____ their dog for a walk.
They _____ just _____ , they were in hysterics.

b This is the past continuous tense. It describes a continuous or unfinished action or state in the past. Find more examples in the story.

c How do we make the past continuous tense?

d Here are two questions in the present continuous tense. Rewrite them in the past continuous tense.

Where is he sitting?
Are they laughing?

2 **Compare the past continuous and the past simple tenses.**

a Complete these sentences from the story.

As I _____ past the lake, I _____ my friends, Carol and Jim.

While we _____ , the dog suddenly _____ up.

b Why are there two different past tenses in these sentences?

We can show the difference like this:

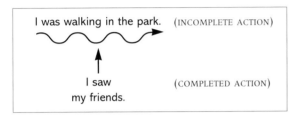

I was walking in the park. (INCOMPLETE ACTION)

I saw (COMPLETED ACTION)
my friends.

c Now look at this sentence. Why are all the verbs in the past simple tense?

When I pulled my hand away, the ice cream flew through the air and it landed on the man's head.

➤ Check the rules for the past continuous tense in **Grammar Reference 6.1**.

Practice

1 **Complete these sentences to make true sentences about the story. Put the verbs in brackets into the past continuous tense.**

1 Carol and Jim _____(walk) through the park.
2 The young woman _____(take) her dog for a walk.
3 Carol and Jim _____(eat) ice creams.
4 The bald man _____(sit) on a bench.
5 He _____(read) a book.
6 Carol and Jim _____(laugh).
7 The bald man _____(laugh).

2 **Make questions to ask the young woman in the story.**

a Write the questions, using this information and the past continuous tense.

1 What/ you/ do
2 What/ Carol and Jim/ do
3 Where/ the bald man/ sit
4 What/ you/ eat
5 Carol and Jim/ eat/ ice cream, too
6 Where/ you/ stand
7 the man/ read/ a book
8 Carol and Jim/ laugh

b Work with a partner. One of you plays the part of the young woman. Ask and answer the questions.

3 **Here is another story of an embarrassing incident.**

a Complete the story. Put the verbs in the box in the past continuous or the past simple tense. Use some verbs more than once.

hide	get into	expect	appear
go	put down	hear	clean
help	ring	fall off	not get dressed
look	run	put on	stand

One afternoon I _____ upstairs to have a bath. As I _____ the bath, the telephone _____ in the hall. I _____ an important call, so I _____ downstairs. There was nobody else at home, so I _____ again. However, while I _____ in the hall with nothing on, I _____ voices outside the front door. It was my teenage daughter and her friends, but I couldn't get back upstairs in time. I _____ the phone, _____ into the living room and _____ behind the curtains. Unfortunately, the window cleaner _____ the living room windows. When I suddenly _____ , the poor man _____ his ladder. Fortunately, when my daughter and her friends _____ the noise, they _____ outside. When I _____ out of the window, they _____ the window cleaner. So I _____ upstairs and _____ a dressing gown. Luckily the window cleaner wasn't hurt, but it was all very embarrassing.

b 🔊 *6.1* Listen and check.

4 **Describe or invent an embarrassing incident from your life.**

a Use this format. What tenses will you use for each of these parts?
• Set the scene: What were you doing? What was happening around you?
• What happened?
• What did you do?

b Read your story to the class.

Reading
The roof of the world

1 Look at the title and pictures.

a What kind of text is it?

b What do you know about this country?

2 Look quickly through the text to find this information.
1 Where is the country?
2 What is its capital city?
3 How many days did the writer spend in the capital?
4 Where did he stay?
5 Approximately how much did the holiday cost?

3 Read the text. Which of these did the report writer do?
- take a sightseeing tour round Kathmandu
- visit the Chitwan National Park
- go by boat through the Trisuli rapids
- go on a trek into the Himalayas
- have a ride on an elephant
- spend seven days in India
- take a flight in a hot air balloon
- fly over Mount Everest
- sleep in a tent
- buy souvenirs

4 How does the holiday in Nepal sound to you?

a Complete the table with information from the text.

positive aspects	negative aspects	neutral aspects

b Compare your ideas with a partner, and then the class.

c What is your idea of the perfect holiday?

5 Write about a real or an imaginary holiday.

a Imagine you are the travel writer for a magazine.

b Write a report on a holiday that you enjoyed, using this format:
- Title
- First impressions
- A day by day account of what you did. Say how you felt about each experience.
- Your general feeling about the holiday
- Advice for other travellers
- Some basic information about costs and flights

Vocabulary file:
Descriptive adjectives and adverbs

The writer uses a lot of adjectives and adverbs to give you a vivid impression of the places and his experiences.

a Underline the adverbs and adjectives in the text which do this.

b Choose three adverbs or adjectives that best describe
- Kathmandu.
- the trek.
- the rapids.
- the holiday in general.

c What does the writer mean by these expressions?
- the roof of the world
- We were entering a different world.
- rich in culture and natural beauty
- white water
- heart-stopping
- Don't expect luxuries.

'I thought we came here to relax!'

Nepal

*A report from the roof of the world by our travel writer, **John Morgan**.*

The ancient buses and cars were hooting loudly, but the cow didn't care. It was sleeping peacefully in the middle of the road and everyone just had to go round it. On the golden roof of a temple some monkeys were playing. In the street people were selling everything from knives to colourful shirts. This was Kathmandu, the capital of Nepal. We were driving from the airport at the start of a week's holiday there, and we were entering a different world.

Between India to the south and Tibet to the north, Nepal is one of the poorest countries in the world, but it is rich in culture and natural beauty, and there is a lot here for the adventurous tourist.

We spent our first day in Kathmandu and took a sightseeing tour around this fascinating city. The Nepalese people are very friendly and there is almost no crime here. But don't expect an exciting night life, because 99 per cent of the population are in bed by 10 pm, and there are no nightclubs.

We needed our sleep, however, because by seven o'clock the next morning we were already travelling to the River Trisuli. Here

The roof of the world!

we began a dramatic journey by boat through the Trisuli rapids. It was heart-stopping – the most exciting experience of my whole life. For mile after mile the white water threw our small boat from side to side. Then suddenly we arrived in the calm water of a beautiful lake.

White water rafting through the Trisuli rapids.

While we were recovering from this amazing experience, our Nepalese guides calmly prepared lunch. Then a minibus took us to Pokhara for our three-day trek into the mountains.

Each day of the trek began at six o'clock. Our guides carried all the equipment and our luggage, prepared all the meals and put up the tents every night. We walked for about 4–6 hours each day through the most spectacular scenery in the world. On day 6 we arrived back in Pokhara for the return flight to Kathmandu. And we spent our final day in Kathmandu buying our souvenirs.

Our seven days in Nepal were wonderful, but don't expect luxuries. In Kathmandu we stayed in the 3-star Marshyangdi Hotel. The rooms were small, but they were clean and had en-suite bathrooms. During the trek we slept in tents, and the toilet was just another tent with a hole in the ground. The food was good, but simple.

There are no direct flights to Kathmandu, so most tours include some time in India. We had three days in India before the week in Nepal and another four days afterwards. These holidays aren't cheap. Prices start at about £1400 per person. ✳

Vocabulary
Places and buildings

1 **Look at this list of places.**

a How many can you find on the map?

church	cathedral
temple	car park
cinema	bank
museum	bus station
railway station	clock tower
castle	park
pub	café
post office	hospital
market	main square
town hall	hotel
supermarket	theatre
library	leisure centre
night club	police station
school	garage

b Arrange the words in a spidergram, like this:

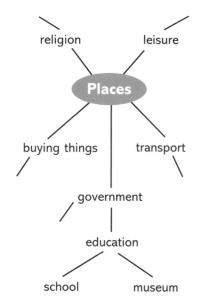

c Can you add any more words to your spidergram?

2 **Think of a village, town or city that you know.**

a Sketch a plan of part of it, putting in the main buildings.

b Explain your plan to a partner.

EXAMPLE

There are lots of cafés in the centre of town. This is my favourite café here. It's opposite the bus station here …

Listening and speaking
Asking the way

1 **You will hear two conversations.**

a 🔊 **6.2** Listen. Where does each person want to get to?

b Find the places on the map.

2 **Can you remember the instructions?**

a Mark the routes on the map.

b 🔊 **6.2** Listen again and check.

Language focus: Giving directions

a Find expressions in tapescript 6.2 to match the diagrams.

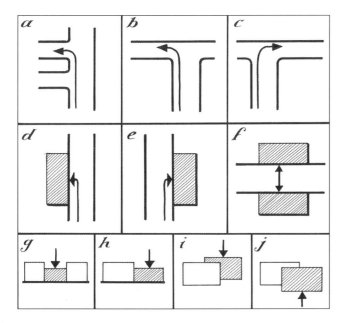

b Work with a partner. Roleplay the conversations, using the tapescript.

3 **Work with a partner. Give directions for these situations, using the map and expressions from the conversations above.**
   1 You are in the car park in Mill Street. Someone asks you the way to the castle.
   2 You are at the station. Someone asks you the way to the hospital.
   3 You are in front of the school. Someone asks you the way to the Post Office.
   4 You are in Carlton Square. Someone asks you the way to the leisure centre.

4 **Work with a partner. You are outside your place of work or study. Ask for and give directions to places in your area.**

'Just keep going round and round at the lights.'

Pronunciation
-a-; word stress

1 The vowel -a-

a The vowel -a- can be pronounced in several different ways.

Look at this list of words. Write them in the correct columns.

castle	again	bald	small
lake	rapid	ancient	way
aren't	calm	water	start
station	saw	today	man
park	natural	hand	final
assistant	came	fat	walk

/æ/	/ɑ:/	/eɪ/	/ɔ:/	/ə/
map	car	radio	all	signal

b 🔲 *6.3* Listen and check.
c 🔲 *6.3* Listen again and repeat.

2 Words with three syllables

a Look at these words with three syllables.

● · · · ● · · · ●
newspaper   together   understand

b Say these words. Mark the syllable with the stress.

photograph	grandmother	inherit
million	financial	genius
assistant	engineer	property
afterwards	argument	difficult
unemployed	expensive	company
relative	introduce	cathedral
possible	dangerous	museum

c 🔲 *6.4* Listen and check.
d Which syllable usually has the stress and which syllable rarely has the stress?

Extension: Reading and listening
It was a normal day ...

1 Here are the beginnings of three stories. Each person is talking about a normal day when something unusual happened.

a Look at these words and phrases.

b Read the stories and write the words and phrases in the correct columns.

telephone	newspaper	roof	wife
cardigan	Sarah Harvey	sofa	windows
tea break	quiz show	radio	meeting
house	husband	bank	

Robin	Katherine	David

2 What do you think happened? Work in groups and complete the stories.

3 Now find out what happened.

a 🔊 **6.5** Listen to the complete stories in the radio programme and compare your ideas.

b Add these words and phrases to the table in **1**.

suitcase	wife and children	green jumper
DJ	bag of tools	cup of tea	safe

4 Discuss these questions.
1 Which story is the most interesting? Why?
2 How do you think the lives of the people changed afterwards?

5 Re-tell one of the stories, using the complete table of words and phrases in **1**.

6 Write your own story (real or imaginary) for *It was a normal day*, using this format:
- Set the scene. What was happening?
- Then what happened?
- How did you feel?
- What did you (or other people) do?
- How did the event change your life?

Language focus: Participles as adjectives

a Complete these sentences from the stories, using these words.

interesting	interested	boring	bored

I'm totally _____ with our marriage.
It was a rather _____ meeting.
Isn't it _____ how you remember these details?
I wanted to talk about it, but he wasn't _____ .

b The adjectives in the box are participles.
Boring is the present participle of the verb *bore*. It describes something that bores you.
EXAMPLE
This programme bores me. It's boring.

Bored is the past participle. It describes how you feel about something.
EXAMPLE
This programme bores me. I'm bored.

c Write the participle adjectives for each of these verbs. Some of them are in the stories. What do the others mean?

worry	shock	stun	interest	bore
excite	frighten	thrill	tire	depress

d Choose the correct adjective for each sentence.
1 Most meetings are *bored/boring*.
2 I feel very *tired/tiring* after that walk.
3 I thought that Robin's story was the most *interested/interesting*.
4 Katherine felt very *depressed/depressing* after her husband left.
5 David's family were *frightened/frightening* by their experience.
6 Why are we so *interested/interesting* in other people's lives?
7 That was a *shocked/shocking* story.

e Work with a partner. Talk about these things, using the adjectives.
EXAMPLES
Horror films are frightening.
I feel frightened when I watch one.

horror films	English	global warming
violence on television		your job or studies
the future	the British Royal Family	

➤ See **Reflecting on Learning 11**: Ways of learning p121.

It was a normal day...

Robin's story

It was nearly ten years ago, so I was about 22. I was working as a builder at the time and I was also the singer with a band in my free time. Anyway, we were building some houses near Farnham in Surrey. It was about half past ten in the morning and most of the other men were having their tea break. They were listening to the radio. I was working on the roof of one of the houses. There was another guy near me. He was painting the windows of the next house.

Katherine's story

It was two years ago now – about eight o'clock in the evening. We were sitting in the living room. My husband was sitting in an armchair. He was reading the paper, as he always did. I was sitting on the sofa. I was knitting. Our daughter was expecting a baby, you see – our first grandchild – and I was knitting a little cardigan for it. Yellow, it was. There was a quiz show on the TV. It was *Strike it Lucky*. Isn't it interesting how you remember these details? But we weren't really watching it. Well, as I said, we were just having a normal evening at home, when suddenly …

David's story

Oh yes, I can remember it as if it was yesterday. I was at work at the time – at the bank. I was having a meeting with my staff. We were all sitting around the big table in my office. It was a rather boring meeting, but most meetings are, I suppose. Anyway, while Sarah Harvey, the assistant manager, was speaking, my secretary came in and said, 'There's a phone call for you.' Well, normally my secretary doesn't interrupt meetings for phone calls. She takes a message. So I was surprised when she came in. 'It's your wife,' she said. 'She says it's urgent.' I was rather worried at this. My wife doesn't panic easily.

Vocabulary
Homophones and homonyms

1 A lot of common words in English have the same sound as another word but a different spelling and meaning. These are called homophones.

EXAMPLES

I   eye

sun   son

a Can you think of any more?

b Correct the spelling mistakes in this conversation.

A I think I've just seen a bare.

B Wear?

A Over their in the would. It was buy that big tree on the write.

B I can't sea anything. But weight a minute. I can here something.

A You're write. But watt is it?

B I don't no.

A Oh, look. I sore it that time.

B It's a dog. The paw thing has hurt itself.

A Yes, it's very week. It's hurt its poor.

2 Words which have the same sound and spelling but a different meaning are called homonyms.

a What different meanings can you find for these words? Use a dictionary to help you.

left	flat	saw	country
play	fine	lift	present

b Make two sentences for each word to illustrate the differences in meaning.

Reading
Where are they now?

1 Read the extract from a magazine and answer these questions.

1 Where is it from?

2 Who is the magazine for?

3 What is this section of the magazine about?

4 What does the editor of the magazine want?

College Life!

Where are they now?

What has happened to former students of Brindley College? Please send any news about yourself or other former students to the editor. This year we have received the following information.

Chris Bowker and Sharon Waring have got married and they have bought a house in York. Chris is still at York University. He has worked there for five years now.

Lesley Miller has gone to work for the Kangaroo Television Company in Sydney. Until last year she worked for BYT Radio in London, but she wanted to try something new. She has been in Australia for six months and she is enjoying every minute of it.

2 Look at the news about former students and answer the questions.

1 What kind of news do you think the magazine normally reports about former students?

2 What news do you think it doesn't publish?

3 Read the two letters to the editor and answer the questions.

1 Who are they from?

2 What is their relationship with the editor?

3 Who do they contain information about?

4 Work in groups. You are the editors of the magazine.

a Discuss these questions.

1 What information do you have about the people in the photographs?

2 Which information would you use for the magazine? Why?

b Put the information that you would use in the table.

Name	Information

```
                                   Flat
                                   14 Ch
                                   Londo
                                   12 No
The Editor
Brindley Bulletin
Brindley College
Exminster
PH8 9QW

Dear Sir or Madam
I have just read the 'Where are they now?' page
of this year's college magazine. I am writing
with some news, as you ask.
The last three years have been very interesting
for me. When I left college I started work with
ICI, but I only stayed there for a year. I had
several temporary jobs and then I got a job
with a record company in London. I have been
here for a year now and am really enjoying it.
I have now bought a flat in Chelsea which is not
very big, but has a magnificent view. I have
been in the flat since September.
Cristina Santorini has gone back to Mexico. She
was working in Birmingham for a couple of years
and I met her at a party. We went out together
for a while, but now she has gone back home.
She has a good job out there, but I cannot
remember what it is.
I hope you can use some of this information in
the next magazine. I enclose a recent
photograph. Thank you for your attention.

Yours faithfully
```

John Marsh

John Marsh

```
                                   27 Chiltern Gardens
                                   Salisbury
                                   SA7 5AM
                                   9 August

Dear Jack,
Hi. It's Fiona. So you're still at Brindley, eh? Well I hope you're
enjoying life.
Here's the latest gossip from me for your 'Where are they now?'
page. I'll start with the most important bit – me. Surprise,
surprise. I've just got married. Yes, it's true. And who's the lucky
man? Well, his name's Michael Kent and I'm madly in love with him.
He's an actor, but you probably haven't heard of him. He works
mostly in the theatre.
We got married in June. But unfortunately, it rained all day. And
my father got as drunk as a skunk. It was so embarrassing! Then
we had a honeymoon in Greece, which was wonderful, simply
wonderful. So, we've been married for eight weeks now – what a
long time!
Now some other news. Zelda and Colin Jackson have just had their
third baby. They've called him Alexander. The twins, Charlotte and
Eric have just started school. Unfortunately, Colin's firm has
closed down, so he's been out of work since June.
But you'll never guess what's happened to Jason Smart. He's in
prison for fraud! He's been there for nearly a year now. I met his
ex-girlfriend a couple of weeks ago and she told me. The funny
thing is, he studied Law at Brindley!
Well, I must close now. Bye for now.
Love from Fiona

P.S. Hope you like the piccy!
```

Language focus:
The present perfect with *for* and *since*

a Look at the sentences and answer the questions.
  He's worked there for five years.
  - Does he work there now?
  He worked there for five years.
  - Does he work there now?

  She's been in Australia for six months.
  - Is she there now?
  She was in Australia for six months.
  - Is she there now?

b Complete the rules with the names of the tenses.

  > - We use the _____ to talk about
  >   an action which started in the past and
  >   continues in the present.
  > - We use the _____ to talk about
  >   an action which started and finished in
  >   the past.

c Look at these two sentences. Translate them.
  *I have been in the flat **since** September.*
  *We've been married **for** eight weeks.*

d Find examples in the letters with *for* and *since*.
  Complete the rule with *for* and *since*.

  > - We use _____ with a period of time.
  > - We use _____ with a point in time.

➤ Check the rules for *for* and *since* in **Grammar Reference 7.2**.

e Complete the phrases with *for* or *since*.

_____ 1994	_____ then
_____ two o'clock	_____ two days
_____ ten years	_____ hours
_____ three minutes	_____ Wednesday
_____ a long time	_____ last week
_____ my birthday	

f Write two sentences about yourself, using *for* and *since*.

5 Write the magazine article. Use the information chart from 4.

6 You are a former student of Brindley College. Write a letter to the editor with news about yourself and two other former students.

Listening and speaking
Meeting visitors

1 **Martin works for a travel company. He is meeting a foreign visitor at the airport.**

a Look at the photographs. What questions do you think he will ask her?

b Look at this list of names.

London	Manchester
Inge Lindstrom	the Grosvenor
the Lake District	William Wordsworth
the Park	the Bombay
Maria Lomas	Windsor Castle

c 🔲 *7.2* Listen to the conversations. Tick (✓) the names you hear.

d Why is each name mentioned in the conversations?

2 **Mark these sentences *True* (✓) or *False* (✗).**
  1 Martin is at the airport when Inge arrives.
  2 He has come to the airport by car.
  3 He offers to carry Inge's suitcase.
  4 Inge has never been to the north of England.
  5 She spent a holiday in London five years ago.
  6 Martin waits at the hotel for her.
  7 Inge has eaten Indian food before.
  8 Martin has never been to the Bombay before.
  9 Inge hasn't seen the programme for her visit yet.
  10 They're going to the Lake District on Saturday.

3 **Can you remember what expressions Martin uses to say these things?**
  • Was the aeroplane journey all right?
  • I'll carry the luggage for you.
  • Are you hungry?
  • Is the hotel room all right?
  • Did you like the food?

a Compare your ideas with a partner.

b 🔲 *7.2* Listen again and check.

4 **Work with a partner. Roleplay the conversations between Martin and Inge, using tapescript 7.2.**

5 **Imagine a foreign visitor is coming to your town.**

a Work with a partner. One of you is the visitor, one is the host. The visitor is coming for a conference, but will have some free time to see things. He/She is arriving by plane at 7.00 pm.

Decide the following:

Host What arrangements have you made for a hotel/a meal/the conference/free time? What questions will you ask to make the visitor feel welcome?

Visitor How do you feel when you arrive? What do you already know about the town or country? What would you like to do in your free time? Do you have any questions about your programme?

b Roleplay the conversation.

Pronunciation
/θ/, /ð/; auxiliary verbs

1 The sounds /θ/ and /ð/

/θ/ and /ð/ are common sounds in English. They are both made with the tip of the tongue against the top front teeth.

/θ/ is voiceless, as in *thin*.

/ð/ is voiced, as in *this*.

a Circle the words with the /θ/ sounds.

sunbathe	mouth	the	bath	these
something	three	weather	that	father
Thursday	tenth	brother	there	with
thousand	both	tooth	throw	thirteen

b 🔲 **7.3** Listen, check and repeat.

2 Auxiliary verbs: strong and weak forms

Some auxiliary verbs (*have, can, do*) are normally unstressed and have a reduced vowel sound. These are called weak forms.

EXAMPLES

/həv/   /kən/
Have you been to New York?   *Can you swim?*

In short answers the auxiliary verb is stressed with the full vowel sound. These are called strong forms.

EXAMPLES

   /hæv/   /kæn/
Yes, I have.   *Yes, I can.*

a Look at the auxiliary verbs in these dialogues. Circle the auxiliary verbs with the strong forms.

1 **A** Are you going to the cinema?
   B Yes, we are.
2 **A** Can I give you a hand?
   B No, it's all right. I can do it.
3 **A** Do you like this programme?
   B Yes, I do.
4 **A** Has John had lunch?
   B Yes, he has.
5 **A** Were the Johnsons going to the party?
   B Yes, they were.
6 **A** How was your trip?
   B It was fine.
7 **A** Was the meal OK?
   B Yes, it was.
8 **A** Can you swim?
   B Yes, I can.

b 🔲 **7.4** Listen and check.

c 🔲 **7.4** Listen again and repeat.

Extension: Reading and listening
Two brothers

1 **Discuss these questions.**

1 Have you ever moved house?
2 Have you ever lived in another country?
3 If not, would you like to do either of these things? Why/why not?

2 **Look at the story and answer the questions.**

1 What are the two brothers' names?
2 Which brother's life does the text describe?
3 What does he think about his life?
4 What does he think about his brother's life?
5 What do the photographs show?

TWO BROTHERS

Emilio and Maximilian are brothers. They are both old men now. They grew up together on a farm in Argentina, but since then they have led very different lives. When Emilio left school at the age of fourteen, he started work on their father's farm. He really enjoyed the simple village life and when their father died, Emilio took over the farm. All his life Emilio has lived in the old farmhouse where he was born. 'I've never wanted to live anywhere else,' he says. 'This is my home. I feel that I'm part of it and it is part of me.'

So for over 70 years Emilio's life has changed very little. When he was 22, he married his childhood sweetheart, Pilar, from the next village, and they have been happily married ever since. Two years ago they celebrated their golden wedding anniversary. It was a big celebration. Everybody from miles around was there, including Emilio and Pilar's six children and their fifteen grandchildren.

Emilio and Pilar have never been abroad. Until he was 60, Emilio went to Buenos Aires once a year, but since his sixtieth birthday he hasn't left the village. 'Well, yes, I've had a good life,' he says, 'but I haven't done very much. Now, look at my brother, Maximilian. He left the village as soon as he had the chance. He hasn't visited us very much in the last twenty years, but we've read about him in the newspapers and we've seen him on TV, too. Yes, Max has had a very interesting life.'

3 **Read the text and mark the sentences** *True (✓),* *False (✗)* **or** *Don't know (?).*

1 Emilio has lived in the same place all his life. ☐
2 He has become very rich. ☐
3 He is 74 years old. ☐
4 He met Pilar when he was twenty years old. ☐
5 He has been married three times. ☐
6 Emilio and Pilar have been married for 52 years. ☐
7 They went to Paris for their honeymoon. ☐
8 Maximilian is a farmer. ☐
9 He is younger than Emilio. ☐
10 He has been on television. ☐
11 He was at the golden wedding. ☐

4 **Make true sentences about the brothers, using this information and the present perfect tense.**
1 Emilio's life/ change/ a lot
2 He/ visit/ the capital city several times
3 Emilio and Pilar/ be married/ over fifty years
4 They/ lead/ a peaceful life
5 They/ be/ United States
6 Emilio/ work/ hard all his life
7 Emilio and Max/ meet/ a long time
8 Emilio/ read/ about Maximilian in the newspapers
9 Max/ do/ a lot of interesting things
10 Emilio/ see/ his brother on television

5 **What do you think Max's life has been like?**

a Here are some things that have played a part in his life. Work in groups and decide Max's life story.

prison	divorce	ship	Wall Street
international jet set		model	travel
car crash	businessman		the Bahamas
drug addict	television		millionaire

b 🔘 **7.5** Listen to the story of Maximilian's life and check your ideas.

6 **Discuss the questions, comparing the lives of the two brothers.**
1 How does each brother feel about his life?
2 Which brother do you think has had the better life?
3 Which brother do you think is happier?
4 Which way of life would you prefer? Why?

7 **Imagine an unusual lifestyle. Here are some ideas.**
- a fashion model
- an actor/actress
- a criminal
- a tycoon
- a tramp

a Work in a group of four. Each person takes a different role. Imagine your life story.

b Take it in turns to be interviewed by the group. The group asks questions to find out as much as possible about your life.

EXAMPLES
How long have you been a …?
Why did you become a …?
How much money have you made as a …?
Have you ever …?
When did you …?

8 **Write the story of your life so far, using this format:**
Describe and give some details about
- what you have done and when you did it.
- where you have lived and when you lived there.
- the main events in your personal life.
Comment on your life. What has it been like so far?

8 Food and health

Grammar
Countables and uncountables; *some* and *any*

Grammar in use

1 Look at the text.

a Answer the questions.
1 What is it about?
2 What is the purpose of the diet?
3 Who is it for?
4 Why is it called the Pyramid diet?

b Read the text and complete the diagram.

2 Discuss these questions.
1 Is the Pyramid diet sensible?
2 Is it appropriate for everyone?
3 Would it provide an interesting diet?

Rules

1 Look at the two groups of words.

a Answer the questions.
1 Which can we make plural?
2 Which can we use *a* or *an* with?

_____ *nouns*	_____ *nouns*
potato apple vitamin	bread pasta calcium

b Write the words *uncountable* and *countable* at the top of the correct columns.

c Find more examples of both types of noun in the text.

➤ Check the rules for countable and uncountable nouns in **Grammar Reference 8.1**.

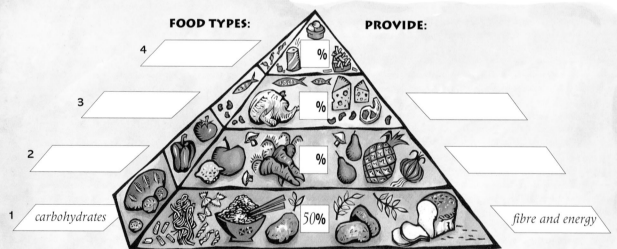

THE PYRAMID

FOOD TYPES: PROVIDE:

4

3

2

1 carbohydrates   50%   fibre and energy

We've had them all – the High Fibre diet, the Protein diet, the Hip and Thigh diet. And here's the latest – the Pyramid diet. But this isn't a diet to help people lose weight. It's a diet for a healthy life. The Pyramid diet is very simple. Different kinds of food are at different levels of the pyramid. The higher up the pyramid, the less you should eat. At the bottom of the pyramid are complex carbohydrates like bread, pasta and potatoes. These provide fibre and energy. About 50% of your diet should be complex carbohydrates. At the second level are fruit and vegetables, such as apples and carrots. These should be about 30% of your diet. They provide vitamins and minerals as well as fibre. Above fruit and vegetables are the protein-rich foods like meat, fish, beans and cheese. These also provide a lot of calcium. These protein-rich foods should be about 18% of your diet. At the top of the pyramid are fat, oil and sugar. We should eat as little as possible of things at this level.

2 When do we use *some*? When do we use *any*?

a  **8.1** Read and listen to this dialogue. Make a rule for using *some* and *any*.

> A *Have you got any money for the parking machine?*
> B *No, I'm sorry. I haven't got any cash on me at all.*
> A *Oh, it's OK. I can get some change at the shop over there.*

b **8.2** Now read and listen to these dialogues.

> A *Are there any apples?*
> B *Yes, but they aren't very good. Shall we get some oranges instead?*
>
> A *Would you like some coffee? I've just made some.*
> B *Oh yes, please. Could I have some sugar in it, please? Thanks.*

c Find examples of *some* and *any*. Are there any that don't follow your rule for **a**?

d Complete the rule.

> We normally use _____ for positive statements and _____ for negative statements and questions. But when a question is an offer, suggestion or request, we usually use _____ , not _____ .

➤ Check the rules for *some* and *any* in **Grammar Reference 8.1**.

Practice

1 Look at this list of words.

| meat | tomato | money | envelope | paint | pencil |
| tea | paper | apples | information | news | equipment |

a Which of these things are uncountable in English?

b Is this the same in your own language?

2 Complete these sentences with *some* or *any*.

1 Can I have _____ more milk, please?
2 Has Jane got _____ brothers or sisters?
3 I haven't got _____ work to do.
4 Is there _____ news about the new project?
5 I've got _____ news for you.
6 There isn't _____ information on the computer about this.
7 Would you like _____ help?
8 Could you get me _____ stamps, please?
9 We went out with _____ friends last night.
10 Is there _____ wine left?

3 Make dialogues like this, using the words in 1.

> A *I need some …*
> B *How much/many do you need?*
> A *Oh, only a little/few.*

4 You have invited two friends to dinner tonight.

a Work with a partner and plan a healthy three-course meal.

b Compare your dinner with other students in the class. Whose dinner is the healthiest?

Vocabulary
Food and drink

1 Look at these different kinds of food and drink.

a Put C (countable) or U (uncountable) beside each one.

b Where does each one go on the pyramid?

tomatoes	yoghurt
ice cream	butter
spaghetti	olive oil
eggs	grapes
nuts	biscuits
rice	peppers
chocolate	prawns
margarine	wine
cucumbers	lemonade
breakfast cereal	chicken
oranges	bananas
salmon	pork
cod	peas
cream	tuna
sausages	beef
ham	apples
noodles	milk
sweets	cakes

c Can you think of any more types of food to add to the pyramid?

2 What do you eat in a typical day?

a Make a list of what you eat and in what quantities.

b Compare your list to the pyramid. What differences are there?

Reading
The Big Man

1 Look at the photographs and the article. Answer these questions.
  1 Who is the man?
  2 Where does he live?
  3 What is his problem?
  4 What is he doing about it?
  5 Is he successful?
  6 How does he want to help other people?

2 Read the article. What significance does each number have in the story?

10	630	28	25	43	250
12–15	96	8	85	9	2

3 Mark these sentences *True* (✓), *False* (✗) or *Don't know* (?).
  1 Walter has lost over 400 kilos in ten months. ☐
  2 His waist measurement is 119 inches. ☐
  3 He used to eat a big breakfast, but he didn't usually eat lunch. ☐
  4 Walter used to spend almost the whole day in bed. ☐
  5 Walter began his diet ten months ago. ☐
  6 He only eats one meal a day now. ☐
  7 Walter is two metres tall. ☐
  8 He still watches TV most of the day. ☐
  9 There are a lot of adverts for food on TV. ☐

The BIG Man

Walter Hudson is big. In fact, he's enormous. He weighs over 250 kilos. And yet Walter is on a diet. He's losing weight at an incredible nine kilos a week. He used to weigh over 630 kilos. That's more than half a ton, and it's heavier than a car or a young elephant. At his maximum size Walter's waist was 119 inches. His neck was as thick as a woman's waist. His biceps were as big as an average man's chest.

His diet was just as impressive. He used to eat enough to feed three families. For breakfast he ate two pounds of sausages, two pounds of bacon, twelve eggs, a pound of biscuits, six Danish pastries, a pot of coffee and four pints of orange juice. Lunch and dinner were even bigger. Then there were the snacks between meals. During the morning he ate twelve doughnuts.

Each afternoon he ate ten large packets of crisps and in the evening a couple of family-sized pizzas. On top of all that he drank 96 cans of soft drinks. That was one day's food and Walter ate that much every day.

Until recently the world knew nothing about Walter Hudson. In the past 28 years he's only been outside for two hours. That was when his family moved house. He hasn't seen the sun since he was 25 years old and he's now 43. He lived in a secret world – a prisoner in his own home near New York. He used to watch television for 12–15 hours a day and he only left his bed to walk the five yards to the bathroom. Even that short journey was exhausting.

Walter's secret world finally hit the headlines ten months ago. He fell over on his way back from the bathroom and became stuck in the doorway. It took eight police officers and firemen to free him.

But that incident changed his life. While he was lying on the floor he decided that enough was enough. The next day he started his diet. He didn't just cut down on food, he stopped eating completely.

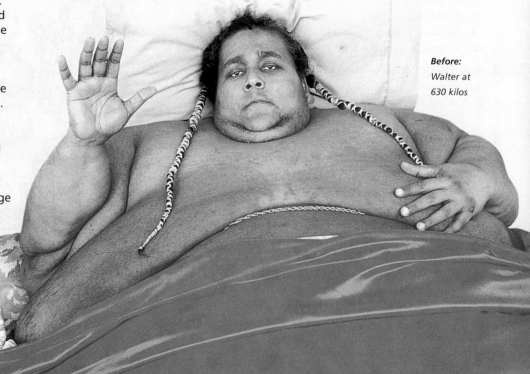

Before:
Walter at 630 kilos

4 Discuss these questions.

1 How do you feel about Walter's story? Do you feel sorry for him?

2 What other kinds of eating disorders or addictions do you know of?

3 What do you think of people with eating problems?

Use these expressions to help you:

It's/It isn't their own fault.
It's because they're weak/greedy/ stupid/unhappy/ill.
We should/n't try to help them.
They need medical attention/ understanding/advice/punishment.
It's the parents'/television's/society's fault.

After: Walter at 250 kilos

Every morning now he drinks a cocktail of vitamins in a pint of orange juice, and during the day he drinks a lot of water. And that's it. He also takes more exercise now. He still has a long way to go, because he wants to get down to 85 kilos. That's the right weight for someone of his height.

'Food,' says Walter, 'is an addiction. It's worse than drugs or alcohol. You can just stop taking them. But you need food. And it's everywhere.' Walter doesn't watch television any more, because too many of the adverts are about food. He hopes that his example will help other overweight people, especially children. He encourages mothers to put photos of him on the fridge door. ' I want parents to say to their kids, "Do you want to look that big? If you keep putting your hands in the fridge, then that's how you'll look. That's what Walter did."'

Vocabulary file: Quantities

To give quantities of uncountable nouns we use a countable expression of quantity.

a Match the expressions to the pictures.

a piece of paper	two bottles of water	a tube of glue
a bag of flour	two cartons of milk	a loaf of bread
a packet of tea	a bar of chocolate	two pounds/
a can of Coke	a jar of marmalade	a kilo of beef

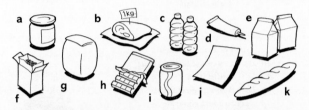

b Find all the words in the text that describe size, quantity or weight and complete the table.

size	quantity	weight

Language focus: *used to*

a Look at these sentences. What does *used to* mean?

Walter used to weigh over 630 kilos, but now he weighs 250 kilos. He used to eat enough for a family, but now he doesn't eat anything. He didn't use to take any exercise, but now he exercises every day.

b How do you think we make questions with *used to*?

➤ Check the rules for *used to* in **Grammar Reference 8.2**.

c What did Walter's life use to be like? Write sentences using this information and *used to*.

weigh	1 19 inches	go outside	drink
eat	watch TV	stay in bed	neck

d Ask other students about their life when they were children. Use this information and *Did you use to ...?*

- have a favourite toy
- Where/ go on holiday
- have a pet
- Where/ live
- What games/ play

- read a lot
- What school subjects/ like best
- argue with your parents
- Who/ play with
- like school

e Write down six things that used to be true about your life. Tell a partner about them and answer your partner's questions.

Listening and speaking
In a restaurant

Starters

soup of the day
melon and Parma ham
fruit juice
prawn cocktail

Main courses

grilled trout with almonds
halibut with cream and tarragon sauce
fillet steak
lamb chops with mint sauce
gammon with pineapple

(all served with a green salad or
fresh vegetables, and French fries or jacket potato)

Desserts

selection of fresh gateaux and desserts
ice cream or sorbet
fresh fruit salad
cheese and biscuits

1 You will hear conversations in a restaurant.

a 8.3 Listen and tick (✓)what they order.

- ☐ an aperitif
- ☐ a starter
- ☐ salad
- ☐ a main course
- ☐ wine
- ☐ dessert
- ☐ coffee/tea
- ☐ brandy

b 8.3 Look at the menu and listen again. What did the people eat? Tick (✓) each person's complete order. What did they have to drink?

Conversation pieces: Ordering a meal

a What do the customers say to
- ask for a table/ the bill/ a receipt?
- order more water?
- refuse dessert?
- ask about the meal?

b What expressions do they use to say these things?
Do you want a drink?
I'll have a mineral water.
Do you want to order now?
I'd like the soup, please.
I'll have the soup and then the lamb chops.

c Look at tapescript 8.3 and check your answers.

2 **Work in groups of three. Roleplay the conversation, using tapescript 8.3.**

3 **Make more conversations in a restaurant.**

a Work in groups of three. One student is the waiter/waitress, two students are the customers. Make conversations using the menu.

b Work with a partner. Take it in turns to be the waiter/waitress and the customer.
Make conversations for these situations:
- The soup is cold.
- You can't decide what to have.
- The bill is too much.
- The waiter brings the wrong order.
- The waiter doesn't speak very good English.
- You order some drinks but the waiter forgets to bring them.

'What year's the mineral water?'

Pronunciation
Silent letters; sentence stress

1 Silent letters

a Some of the words in this list have a silent letter. Circle the silent letters.

calm	walk	bald	thumb	bomb	lamb
wrong	write	white	knee	knife	know
yoghurt	spaghetti	halibut	hotel	hour	
honest	kept	receipt	accept	salmon	

b 📼 *8.4* Listen, check and repeat.

2 Sentence stress

English is a stress-timed language. Unstressed syllables are made longer or shorter to fit between the main stresses in a sentence.

a 📼 *8.5* Listen to this sentence.

●　●　●　●　●　●　●　●　●　●

When am I seeing you for lunch next week?

In this sentence there are four main stresses. The interval between each stress is the same. But how many syllables are there between

- stresses 1 and 2?　_____
- stresses 2 and 3?　_____
- stresses 3 and 4?　_____

b 📼 *8.6* Listen to these dialogues.

1 A Do you like these trousers?

　B Yes, I do.

2 A Where's my pen?

　B It's on the desk.

3 A What's the time?

　B It's quarter to eleven.

4 A When's the meeting?

　B I'll give you a ring.

c Each sentence has two main stresses. Mark them.

d 📼 *8.6* Listen again and check your ideas.

e 📼 *8.6* Listen again and repeat.

Extension: Reading and listening
How long could you live?

1 Look at the questionnaire.

a Read the introduction and answer the questions.
1 What is the questionnaire about?
2 What things depend on luck?
3 What is the questionnaire based on?

b Complete the questionnaire.

c Compare answers with your partner. What differences are there?

d What effect do you think your answers will have on your life expectancy?

How **long** could you live?

What is your life expectancy? A lot depends on luck – whether you have an accident and who your grandparents are. But you can also control some things in your lifestyle. So how long could you live? This questionnaire is based on life insurance tests.

Write your answers in the spaces.

Score
+ / –

1   Are you male or female?

2   How old are you?

3   Do you live in an urban area with a population of more than 2 million people?

4   Do you live in a rural area with less than 10,000 inhabitants?

5   Do you live alone?

6   Do you live with a partner (husband/wife, boyfriend/girlfriend)?

7   Do you or will you have a university degree?

8   Do you or will you have a postgraduate degree or a similar professional qualification?

9   Do you or will you have a sedentary job?

10   How often do you jog, swim, play a sport or take similar exercise?

11   Do you usually sleep for more than 10 hours a day?

2 **You will hear how to calculate your life expectancy.**

a 🔲 *8.7* Listen and write down what you must add or subtract in the boxes on the right-hand side.

EXAMPLE

Add 4   *+ 4*

Subtract 3   *– 3*

b 🔲 *8.7* Listen again and check your scores.

c Calculate your life expectancy.

Doctors say that if you get married, don't smoke, don't drink, don't eat too much, don't stay up late and don't drive a fast car, you will live longer. But this isn't true. You don't really live longer. It just seems like it.

12 Are you happy?

13 Are you generally relaxed or do you lose your temper easily?

14 How many cigarettes (if any) do you smoke a day?

15 How much alcohol (if any) do you drink a day?

16 Are you overweight? If so, by how much?

17 How old are your grandparents, or how old were they when they died?

18 Does anyone in your family suffer from heart disease?

Total life expectancy:

3 **Complete the table with the information about your life expectancy.**

the things that increase my life expectancy	the things that reduce my life expectancy
I don't smoke.	*I'm male.*

4 **Find words or expressions with the same meaning from the questionnaire or tapescript.**

1 He *loses his temper easily.*
2 Too much *wine and beer* is bad for you.
3 I've got *a job where I sit down most of the time.*
4 *Subtract* 2 years if you're *not happy.*
5 You'll live longer if you're *a person who doesn't smoke,* but not if you live with *someone who smokes.*
6 Do you live *alone*?
7 You live longer if you're *a woman* than if you're *a man.*
8 Life in *urban areas* is less healthy than life in *rural areas.*
9 If you're *overweight,* you're more likely to *suffer from heart disease.*
10 Long life *is hereditary.*
11 This town has *a population of 10,000 people.*
12 How well do you know your *husband or boyfriend*?

5 **Discuss these questions with other members of the class.**

1 Do you agree with the calculations?
2 What aspects of your lifestyle put you at risk?
3 What can you do to reduce the risks?
4 Do you want to keep your lifestyle even if it increases the risks?

Use these expressions:

According to the tape …
The tape says that …
I (don't) agree with this, because …
I think that … is(n't) good for you.
I will increase my life expectancy if I …

- *stop smoking*
- *lose weight*
- *move to the country*
- *take more exercise*
- *drink less*
- *try to be more relaxed*
- *get married*

9 Possibilities

Grammar
would; second conditional

Grammar in use 1

1 Look at the speech bubbles. Are the people talking about a real or an imaginary situation?

> What *would your ideal day be* like?
> What *would you do*?
> What *wouldn't you do*?

> *I'd spend* the day on the beach.

> *I wouldn't get up* till midday.

> *I would tell* my boss that he's a boring old fool.

2 Do you agree with any of the ideas?

Rules

1 The verbs in the dialogues above are in the conditional verb form.
a Find these forms:
- a positive statement (long form)
- a positive statement (short form)
- a negative statement
- a question
b What do you think the long form of the negative is?
➤ Check the rules for *would* in **Grammar Reference 9.1**.

Practice

1 Think about your ideal day. Would you do these things? Tell your partner.

EXAMPLE
I'd/wouldn't get up early.

> get up early   have a party   go to work   watch TV   stay in bed
> visit friends   go to the theatre   spend time with your family

2 What other things would/wouldn't you do? Talk about them with your partner and the class.

Grammar in use 2

1 What is the questionnaire about?

2 Answer the questions.

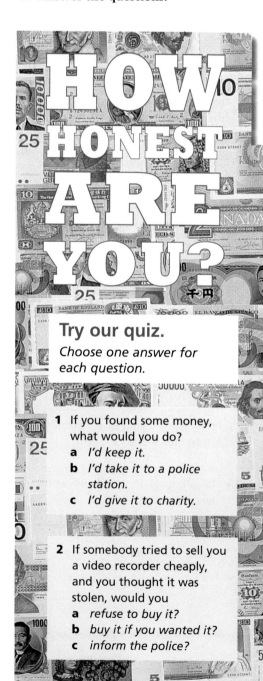

HOW HONEST ARE YOU?

Try our quiz.
Choose one answer for each question.

1 If you found some money, what would you do?
  a *I'd keep it.*
  b *I'd take it to a police station.*
  c *I'd give it to charity.*

2 If somebody tried to sell you a video recorder cheaply, and you thought it was stolen, would you
  a *refuse to buy it?*
  b *buy it if you wanted it?*
  c *inform the police?*

Rules

1 The questionnaire uses the second conditional.

a Complete this sentence from the questionnaire.

If you _____ some money, what _____ you do?

b What form of the verb is used
- in the *if* clause?
- in the main clause?

2 When do we use the second conditional?

a Look at these sentences.

If they offer me the job, I'll take it.
If someone offered me a job, I'd take it.

Which sentence is talking about:
- a real situation?
- an imaginary situation?

b Which tenses are used?

➤ Check the rules for the second conditional in **Grammar Reference 9.2**.

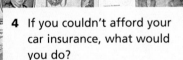

3 If you saw your friend trying to steal something from a shop, would you
   a *do nothing?*
   b *tell your friend to put it back?*
   c *tell a shop assistant?*

4 If you couldn't afford your car insurance, what would you do?
   a *The car would stay in the garage until I had enough money.*
   b *I'd drive the car anyway.*
   c *I wouldn't drive it except in an emergency.*

5 If a shop assistant gave you too much change, what would you do?
   a *I'd say nothing and take the money.*
   b *I'd tell the shop assistant if I thought that he/she would get into trouble.*
   c *I'd give it back to the shop assistant.*

Practice

1 Compare your answers to the questionnaire with a partner.

EXAMPLE
A What would you do if you found some money?
B I'd …
A So would I./I wouldn't. I'd …

2 How would a psychologist analyse your answers?

a Discuss your ideas with your partner.

b 📟 *9.1* Listen to a psychologist analysing the possible questionnaire results and check your answers. Were you right?

c The psychologist says, 'For most people, a lot would depend on the circumstances.' Look again at your answers. In what circumstances would you give a different answer?

3 What is the first thing that you would do in these imaginary situations?

EXAMPLE
If I was ruler of the world, I'd ban nuclear weapons.

- You are ruler of the world.
- Your house catches fire.
- You see a car crash.
- You win the national lottery.
- You become head of your country.
- You are the boss of your company/college/school.
- You're in a bank when a robbery happens.

4 Think of three more hypothetical situations. Ask students in the class what they would do.

5 Match a clause in A and a clause in B.

A	B
If I found a credit card,	I'll be very happy.
I'll play the guitar	if I see him.
If it's sunny tomorrow,	I wouldn't use it.
I'll tell him your news	if you sing.
I'd go round the world	she'd be very happy.
If Sarah got the job,	if I was rich.

6 Complete the sentences with your own ideas.

1 If I found £1,000, _____ .
2 _____ I'd be very sad.
3 If it rains this weekend, _____ .
4 If you study hard, _____ .
5 _____ if you don't hurry.
6 _____ if I was Prime Minister.

7 Write a questionnaire.

a Work in groups. Think of another topic for a questionnaire. Here are some ideas.
- How sensitive are you?
- How hot-tempered are you?
- How optimistic/pessimistic are you?

b Write some questions and work out the questionnaire results.

c Try out your questionnaire on another group.

Vocabulary
Crime

1 **Look at this list of crimes.**

a Use a dictionary to help you. Which are

- crimes against people?
- crimes against property?

murder	assault	robbery
theft	shoplifting	blackmail
kidnapping	burglary	vandalism

b Write the crimes in the first column in the table.

c Use a dictionary. Find the words for the next two columns.

crime	criminal	action
murder	murderer	to murder
assault	attacker/ mugger	to attack/ to mug

d Which crimes would you associate these words with?

shoot	break into	threaten
money	knife	hit	gun
grab	smash	stab

Reading
Would you get involved?

1 **Look at the title. What do you think the text is about?**

a Read the first paragraph. What advice would you expect the police to give?

b Read the rest of the text and answer the questions.

  1 What happened to each of these people?
  - Dave Johnson
  - Pauline Castle
  - James Bulger
  - Kitty Genovese
  - Dave Greenwood

  2 What do the police advise?

2 **Read the text again.**

a Find three reasons why people do not get involved.

b Which case illustrates each of the reasons?

c Discuss these questions.
  1 What do you think about each of the cases?
  2 What would you do in each of these cases?
  3 What do you think of the police advice?

3 **Work in groups to discuss these questions. Then compare your answers with the class.**

  1 Would you get involved if
  - a car was on fire and there were people inside?
  - two people were assaulting someone?
  - a thief grabbed someone's bag?
  - two young men were breaking into a car?

  2 Would it make any difference if the victim was
  - a member of your family?
  - a neighbour?
  - a colleague?
  - a stranger?
  - a child?
  - a woman?
  - a man?

  3 Have you ever witnessed a crime or a dangerous incident? What did you do?

  4 Have you had an experience that made you think: 'I wouldn't do it again'? What happened?

4 **Here is an incident that happened to Peter Morris.**

a Describe what happened, using the information.

b Add an ending and say how the experience changed Peter's attitude. What would he do next time?

Peter Morris/ drive along road
lonely road/ evening
car/ stopped by side of the road
woman/ looking at engine
Peter/ stop to help
man/ appear from car/ point gun at Peter
steal wallet/ take Peter's car/ drive away

Would you get involved?

What would you do if you saw a robbery or an assault? Would you intervene? If your neighbour's house was on fire, would you try to rescue the people inside? What would you do if someone needed your help in a dangerous situation? Would you get involved?

Dave Johnson was walking home one night when he saw a house on fire. Someone inside was shouting for help. 'I couldn't just stand there and do nothing,' says Dave. 'I broke down the door and went in. It was extremely hot and there was smoke everywhere. But I got the old man out. Two minutes later the whole house was in flames. Yes, I'd do the same thing again.'

But Pauline Castle would not get involved again. She intervened to help a neighbour when she heard a noise in the street. Pauline explains what happened. 'Two girls were throwing stones at my neighbour's house. I shouted at them. But then they came over to my house and threatened me. I was shocked and really frightened. They were only about thirteen years old. I wouldn't do it again. I'd just ignore it. In fact last week I saw some boys vandalizing an empty shop in the next street, but I didn't do anything. I just crossed the street. No, I wouldn't get involved again. It's not worth it.'

Pauline's experience changed her attitude. In many other cases people would not intervene because they are afraid that they would look silly if they were wrong. In a famous case in 1993 two twelve-year-old boys murdered a little boy called James Bulger. Over a hundred witnesses saw James with the two boys before the murder. The boys were pushing him and hitting him. But all the witnesses thought that he was with his brothers, so they did not do anything.

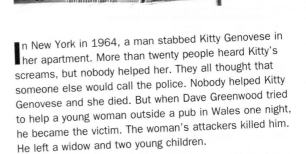

In New York in 1964, a man stabbed Kitty Genovese in her apartment. More than twenty people heard Kitty's screams, but nobody helped her. They all thought that someone else would call the police. Nobody helped Kitty Genovese and she died. But when Dave Greenwood tried to help a young woman outside a pub in Wales one night, he became the victim. The woman's attackers killed him. He left a widow and two young children.

It is because of cases like this that the police say: 'Don't be a hero. Dial 999 and leave it to the police or the fire brigade.' But in the heat of the moment, if someone was in trouble, what would you do?

Listening and speaking
Checking into a hotel

1 Look at the photograph. A guest is checking into a hotel. Imagine the conversation with the receptionist.

a What words and expressions would you hear?

b What would they say to each other?

c 📼 *9.2* Listen and check your ideas.

2 Look at the conversation.

a Work with a partner and complete the conversation with these words.

> wake-up call   number   suitcase   sign   imprint
> registration   single   lift   name   nights   bill   key
> reservation   luggage   credit card   stay   minute

Receptionist   Good evening, sir.

Guest   Good evening. Do you have a _____ in the _____ of Jones, please?

Receptionist   Just a _____ , sir. Yes, here we are. Mr Alan Jones. Would you like a _____ room or a double, Mr Jones?

Guest   I'd prefer a double, if you've got one.

Receptionist   And how many _____ are you staying?

Guest   Three.

Receptionist   Fine. Well, could you just fill in the _____ form and _____ it at the bottom, please?

Guest   Yes, certainly.

Receptionist   And how do you want to settle the _____?

Guest   By _____ , if that's all right.

Receptionist   Yes, of course. Could I just take an _____ of the card, sir?

Guest   Yes, here you are.

Receptionist   Thank you. And will you require a newspaper and a _____ in the morning?

Guest   Yes, I'd like *The Times* and a call at 7.30, please.

Receptionist   7.30. Very good, sir. Here's your _____ . Your room _____ is 429. The _____ is over there. Do you need any help with your _____?

Guest   No, thank you. I've only got a small _____ .

Receptionist   Well, enjoy your _____ .

Guest   Thank you.

b 📼 *9.2* Listen and check your answers.

3 Work with a partner. Roleplay the conversation.

Conversation pieces:
Polite requests

a Look at these expressions.

Could you (just) …?
Could I (just) …?

Just makes the request sound more polite.
These expressions are usually followed by *please*.

b Find the expressions in the conversation. How do the people respond to the requests?

c Work with a partner. Take it in turns to make the following requests and respond.

EXAMPLE

Could you just sign the form at the bottom, please?
Yes, certainly.

Ask someone to
- sign the form at the bottom.
- excuse you, while you make a telephone call.
- get your suitcases from your car.
- see if there are any messages for you.
- put your bag in the room.
- send a fax for you.

Ask if you can
- borrow a pen.
- see someone's passport.
- check the bill.
- make a phone call.
- leave your bags there.
- cancel your wake-up call.

d Look at your requests. Who would make them, guest or receptionist?

4 **Work with a partner. Take it in turns to be the guest and the receptionist. Make new conversations with this information.**

- single room/ one night/ voucher/ *Herald Tribune*/ 6.45/ one suitcase in the car

- double room/ a week/ send bill to company/ no newspaper/ 7.15/ two suitcases

Pronunciation
-ou-; emphatic stress

1 The vowels *-ou-*

The vowels *-ou-* can be pronounced in many different ways.

a Look at this list of words. Put them into the correct column.

encourage   flour   thought   pound   our   enough   bought
couple   trouble   double   fought   would   voucher   country
out   you   should   round   could   house   your   through

/ɔː/	/ʊ/	/uː/	/ʌ/	/aʊ/

b 9.3 Listen, check and repeat.

2 Emphatic stress

When we want to emphasize certain information in a sentence, we stress that part.

a 9.4 Listen to this sentence. The stress can go on three different parts.

   1   2   3
We need to be at the meeting at three o'clock.

The different stresses change the meaning.

b Match the meanings below to the stress points 1, 2, and 3.

☐ The meeting is at three, not four.
☐ You and I have to be there at three, but the others don't.
☐ We need to be at the meeting at three, so we must arrive at the building earlier.

c 9.5 Listen to the first part of these sentences. Mark the main stress.

d Choose the correct ending for each sentence.

1 I live at number 11 Johnson Road, | not my brother.
                                                 | not number 12.
                                                 | not Johnson Close.

2 Alison used to be a singer, | not a piano player.
                                       | but she isn't now.
                                       | not Jane.

3 The news is on Channel 1 now, | not later.
                                       | not *Dallas*.
                                       | not Channel 3.

4 It'll be sunny tomorrow afternoon, | not rainy.
                                       | not tomorrow morning.
                                       | not this afternoon.

5 Your books are on the table, | not in the cupboard.
                                       | not your pen.
                                       | not mine.

e 9.6 Listen to the sentences and check your answers.

f 9.6 Listen again and repeat.

Extension: Reading and listening
Smart shopping

1 Look at the pictures.

a What do you think the article is about?

b What is happening in each picture?

c Put the pictures in the correct order.

d Read the article and check your order.

2 Discuss these questions.

1 Would you like to shop in a smart store?

2 What do you think the advantages and disadvantages of the smart store would be
   • for the stores?
   • for the staff?
   • for the customers?

3 You will hear someone talking about the advantages and disadvantages of smart stores.

a ▭ 9.7 Listen and note down the points.

b Compare them to your own ideas.

Smart Shopping

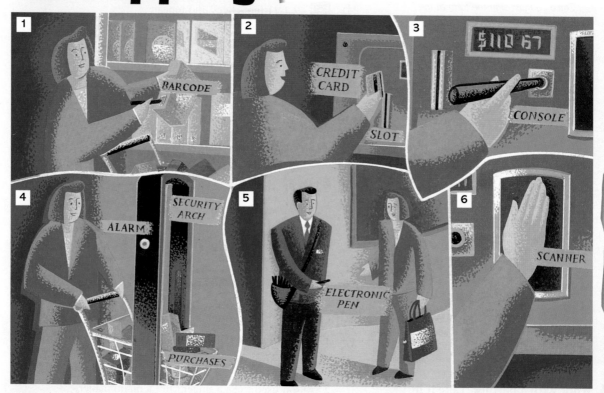

Shopping at the supermarket can be a real chore. And what do shoppers hate most about it? – queues at the checkout. But they wouldn't need to queue if supermarkets used the latest idea in shopping.

This idea is the 'smart store'. The smart store would replace checkout assistants with computer technology, and queues at the checkouts would disappear. How

would the smart store work? When you entered the smart supermarket, you'd collect a small electronic pen from an assistant. Then you'd go round the store as you normally do and take things from the shelves. You'd run the pen over the bar code on the goods before you put them in your trolley, and the pen would record your purchases. At the checkout, you wouldn't meet a checkout assistant, instead you'd find a checkout console. You'd put the

pen into the console and the computer in the console would show the total cost. To pay, you'd pass a credit card through a slot on the console. Then you'd put your hand or finger on a scanner. This would identify you, so you couldn't use someone else's credit card. You'd leave the shop through a security arch like the ones at airports. If you didn't scan everything in your trolley, an alarm would ring. **£**

4 **Here is another idea for smart shopping.**

a Look at the information and the pictures. How would it work?

EXAMPLE

You would run the pen over the bar codes on the goods in the cupboard or fridge.

b What do you think the advantages and disadvantages of it would be?

c Continue the description of smart shopping from home, using this format:
- Introduction
- How would it work?
- What would be the advantages?
- What would be the disadvantages?

Smart shopping from home

Many people don't like shopping at supermarkets, but you wouldn't need to go to the supermarket if you used the latest idea in home shopping. You wouldn't even leave your own home. How would it work?

You'd need an electronic pen from your supermarket. You'd go to your cupboard or fridge and you'd run the pen over the bar codes on the things that you wanted to buy. The pen would record what you wanted. Then you'd go to your telephone. You'd ....

1 pen/ bar codes/ cupboard or fridge
  pen/ record/ what you want

2 pen/ console on telephone

3 dial/ store number

4 telephone/ send/ order/ store

5 store/ pack/ order

6 store/ deliver/ order

10 Activities

Grammar
going to

Grammar in use

1 Discuss these questions.
  1 Do you ever make New Year's resolutions?
  2 Do you keep them?
  3 What do you think are the most common resolutions?
  4 Why do people make resolutions and then not keep them?

2 Look at the cartoon.

a Read the story and decide what the New Year's Resolution is going to be.

b Compare your ideas with the class.

c 🔲 *10.1* Listen to the story and check.

Rules

1 Look at the cartoon again.

a Find these forms of *going to*:
  • a positive sentence
  • a negative sentence
  • a question

b How do we make these forms?

The New Year's Resolution

HAPPY NEW YEAR

This year, Karen, I'm going to give up smoking. It won't be easy. But I'm not going to touch another cigarette.

You won't give up. You make a resolution every year, but you never keep it.

I know, I'll give up, too. Then we can keep an eye on each other.

Great idea, John.

Hmm.

It's all right. We won't have any more.

Mm, no, we won't.

February

Happy New Year, Mike. Are you going to break your New Year's resolution again this year?

No, this year I'm going to keep it.

A year later

And why is this year different?

Because this year I'm _____.

2 When do we use *going to* to talk about the future?

a Look at these sentences from the story. Say which future form is used and why.

> *Mike*   *This year, Karen, I'm going to give up smoking.*
> *Karen* *You won't give up smoking.*
> *John*   *I'll give up, too.*

b Use the sentences to complete the examples for the rules.

We use *will*

- to make predictions or talk about the future in general.

  EXAMPLE

  _____

- when we decide to do something at the moment of speaking.

  EXAMPLE

  _____

We use *going to*

- to talk about something that we have already decided to do.

  EXAMPLE

  _____

---

c Find one more example of each use in the story.

➤ Check the rules for *going to* in **Grammar Reference 10.1**.

Practice

1 What are this family's resolutions?

a Make sentences with *going to* and this information.

EXAMPLES

My husband's going to go on a diet.
He isn't going to drink so much beer.

I / take / exercise
I / work / hard

My son / have / haircut
He / watch / TV

My daughter / tidy / bedroom
She / talk / phone for hours

We / be nicer to each other
We / argue with each other

b 🔊 *10.2* Listen and check.

2 The rest of your life starts here!

a Make three resolutions to improve your life or to fulfil your ambitions.

b Work with a partner. Tell your partner about your resolutions and answer any questions that your partner asks.

c Change partners. Tell your new partner about your first partner's resolutions.

3 Choose the correct future form for each sentence.

1 **A** John and I **are going to / will** get married.
    B Oh that's great news!

2 **A** I can't find my wallet!
    B **I'm going to / I'll** help you look for it.

3 **A** Shall we go out for a meal this evening?
    B Yes, OK. **I'm going to / I'll** phone and book a table.

4 Can you record that programme for me? **I'm going to / I'll** have a bath.

5 **A** It's my birthday on Saturday.
    B **Are you going to / Will you** have a party?

6 **A** I'm going to get a cup of coffee.
    B Good idea. **I'm going to / I'll** get one, too.

7 **A** Here's that report.
    B Oh, thanks. **I'm going to / I'll** read it this evening.

8 If you see a black cat, **you're going to / you'll** have good luck.

4 Go round the class. Find out about people's plans for

- after the class.
- this evening.
- tomorrow.
- the weekend.
- next Tuesday.
- the summer.
- their next holiday.

EXAMPLE

What are you going to do … ?

If you already have plans say:

I'm/We're going to …

If you are not sure, say:

Perhaps I/We'll …
or *I don't know. I/We'll probably …*

Vocabulary
Gerunds; activities

1 **Look at this list of activities. Which do you like doing?**

> playing football   having a shower   sitting   writing   jogging
> sunbathing   digging the garden   cycling   shopping   skating
> skipping   sleeping   shaving   knitting   getting dressed
> swimming   doing housework   dancing   driving   washing up

2 **The words in 1 are all gerunds.**

a A gerund is the *-ing* form of a verb. How do we make the gerunds of these verbs?

> play   sleep   cycle   shave   skip   knit

b A gerund is a noun. We use it as the subject or object of a sentence, and following a preposition. What types of gerund are in these sentences?

> *I like **swimming**.*
> *She's very good at **swimming**.*
> ***Swimming** is good for you.*

3 **Look at the chart. What does it show?**

a [cassette] *10.3* Listen to some information about the activities above.

b Put the activities above in the correct category.

How many calories can you burn in one hour?		
Type of activity	Calories	Examples
rest	60	*reading,* _____
very light activities	75	*eating,* _____
light activities	100	*playing the piano,* _____
moderate activities	100–200	*walking,* _____
energetic activities	200–400	*horse riding,* _____
strenuous activities	400–600	*climbing stairs,* _____

c [cassette] *10.3* Listen again and check your answers.

4 **Look at these activities.**

a Which category do you think they go in? Discuss your ideas.

> fishing   ironing   cleaning a car   weightlifting
> looking after children   sailing   travelling by plane
> running   cooking   skiing   singing
> breathing   windsurfing   sewing

b How many energetic or strenuous activities do you do?

➤ Check the rules for gerunds in **Grammar Reference 10.2**.

Reading
The £349 housewife

1 **Look at the picture and the headline of the article.**

a What do you think the article is about?

b The first paragraph mentions £349 and 71 hours. What do you think these numbers represent?

c Look at the text and check your ideas.

d Look at the chart. Find the job titles for these activities.

> washing up   preparing meals
> washing clothes   sewing
> looking after children

2 **Read the text. Mark these sentences *True (✓), False (✗), or Don't know (?)*.**

1 The average housewife works nearly 71 hours a week. ☐
2 Seventy per cent of the working population earn £18,000 a year. ☐
3 Train drivers earn the same as prison officers. ☐
4 Teachers earn about £24,000 a year. ☐
5 Looking after children takes up most time. ☐
6 Wives with jobs spend more time on housework than on their jobs. ☐
7 The average mother with a child under one works 95 hours a week. ☐
8 Karen Tudor-Williams thinks that the government should pay women wages. ☐
9 Her husband helps with a lot of the housework. ☐
10 Anne Neale thinks that husbands' employers should pay housewives. ☐

3 **Discuss these questions.**

1 How do you feel about the situation in the text?
2 Do you think the situation is similar in your country?
3 Do you agree with Karen and Anne? What, if anything, should be done about the situation?

The £349 housewife

How her weekly pay slip would add up...

		£ hr	£ week
Nanny	17.9 hrs	£5.50	£105.95
Cook	12.2 hrs	£5.35	£65.27
Cleaner	12.2 hrs	£5.35	£65.27
Laundress	9.3 hrs	£3.80	£35.34
Shopper	6.4 hrs	£3.80	£24.32
Dishwasher	5.7 hrs	£3.80	£21.66
Driver	2.6 hrs	£4.50	£11.70
Gardener	1.4 hrs	£5.90	£8.26
Seamstress	1.7 hrs	£3.60	£6.12
Other tasks	1.3 hrs	£4.00	£5.20
Total	**70.7 hrs**		**£349.09**

As nanny, cook, cleaner, laundress, shopper, dishwasher, driver, gardener, and seamstress, she has one of the most demanding jobs in Britain today. And paying someone else to do the chores which take the average housewife 71 hours a week would cost £349, it was revealed yesterday.

At over £18,000 a year that's more than the earnings of 70 per cent of the population, including train drivers, firemen, prison officers, and social workers.

Looking after a youngster less than a year old takes a housewife into an even higher pay league. According to a survey, she deserves £457 a week – at nearly £24,000 a year, the same as teachers, engineers, and chemists.

By SEAN POULTER

Researchers put a price on each chore, then calculated how long the average person takes doing them. They found housewives spend an average 70.7 hours a week on domestic duties – with looking after the children (17.9 hours) and cooking and cleaning (12.3 hours each) the most time-consuming.

A wife with a part-time job still works an average of 59 hours a week at home. Those in full-time employment put in longer hours at home than in the workplace.

The good news is that these hours decline sharply as children get older. While the average mother with a child under one puts in 90 hours weekly, the figure drops to 80 hours from one to four and to 66 hours from five to ten.

Mother-of-four Karen Tudor-Williams, from Reading, said last night: 'Wages aren't practical, but the government should recognize the value of housework, perhaps through the tax system. Running a house takes a lot of time and most husbands don't appreciate this. They say they do the DIY jobs, but my husband only puts a shelf up now and again. He never cleans the loo – that's the real test.'

Single parent Anne Neale from North-west London said: 'The Government should pay women wages. It's the husband's employer who benefits from the work that women do at home.'

Listening and speaking
Making suggestions

1 **You will hear three conversations.**

a Look at the list of possible activities.

b 🔲 *10.4* Listen and match each conversation with an activity.

Conversation 1	visiting relatives
	going to a restaurant
	booking a holiday
Conversation 2	watching a video
	going to a wedding
	spending a day in the country
Conversation 3	having a game of tennis
	planning a party

2 **Look at this list of activities.**

a Tick (✓) the activities that the people are going to do.

- ☐ go to the beach
- ☐ have a picnic by the river
- ☐ invite some friends from Spain
- ☐ telephone Diane and Peter
- ☐ eat at the Red Dragon restaurant
- ☐ try the new Italian restaurant
- ☐ book a table at Mario's
- ☐ go to the cinema
- ☐ hire a video
- ☐ have a bath
- ☐ phone the video shop
- ☐ get some pizzas

b 🔲 *10.4* Listen again and check your answers.

Conversation pieces: Expressions with -ing forms

Some of the expressions in the conversations use the -ing form of the verb. Some use the infinitive without to.

a Complete these expressions with the correct form of the verb go.

b Look at tapescript 10.4 and check your answers.

c Practise the conversations with a partner.

➤ You can go to the Pronunciation section first for practice.

Making suggestions:

How about
What about   _____
Do you fancy   *for a picnic?*
Shall we   _____
Why don't we   _____
Would you like to   _____

We could   _____   *swimming.*
Let's

Expressing likes/dislikes/preferences:

I | *don't fancy* | _____ *to the cinema.*
    | *don't mind* |

I | *like* |
    | *love* |
    | *enjoy* | _____ *to the video shop.*
    | *prefer* |
    | *hate* |
    | *can't stand* |

I'd rather _____ *shopping.*

Asking people to do things:

Would you mind   _____
Could you   *to the shops for me, please?*
Do you think you could _____

3 Look at these suggestions for things to do.

a Work with a partner. Think of a possible objection to each.
- go to that new Indian restaurant
- watch the football on TV
- do some gardening
- have a party next week
- invite some friends round
- play tennis
- go for a drink
- have a barbecue
- hire a video
- go swimming

b Make conversations like this, using the expressions above.
A Make a suggestion.
B Object and make another suggestion.
A Accept the new suggestion. Ask B to do something.

EXAMPLE
A How about going to that new Indian restaurant tonight?
B No, I don't fancy eating Indian food. Why don't we go to the Oasis?
A OK. Do you think you could book a table?

c Have conversations about these situations.
- arranging a day out
- planning a party
- deciding what to do this evening

Pronunciation
/tʃ/, /ʃ/; suggestions

1 The sounds /tʃ/ and /ʃ/

a 🔊 *10.5* Listen and tick (✓) the word you hear.

watch	wash	cheap	sheep
catch	cash	chew	shoe
chop	shop	which	wish
chip	ship	choose	shoes

b Say these sentences.
Which watch did she choose?
Watch while I wash these cheap shoes.
She was chatting to the shy children at the chip shop.

c 🔊 *10.6* Listen, check and repeat.

2 Making suggestions

We can use questions or statements for making suggestions. They follow the normal intonation patterns.

a Say these with the correct intonation.
Wh- questions:

What shall we do tonight?
Yes/No questions:

Shall we go to the movies?
Statements:

Let's go out for a meal.

b 🔊 *10.7* Listen, check and repeat.

c Mark these suggestions with the correct intonation.

1 Do you fancy going out tonight?

2 Let's go to the beach.

3 What about getting a video?

4 Shall we book a table at the bistro?

5 Do you want to go to the party?

6 Why don't we try that new pub?

7 I fancy seeing a film tonight.

8 How about spending a week in Rio?

d 🔊 *10.8* Listen, check and repeat.

e Practise saying the sentences.

Extension: Listening and speaking
The pleasure principle

1 Here is the introduction to a radio interview.

a 📼 *10.9* Read and listen to the introduction.

> '"Pleasure is the beginning and the end of living happily." Those are the words of the Greek philosopher Epicurus, who lived 2300 years ago. People have always tried to find pleasure and today we have many more pleasures than the Ancient Greeks had. And yet we still don't know a lot about this important part of life. Here in the studio is Dr Jonathan Shamberg. Good evening, Dr Shamberg.'

b Discuss these questions.
1 What will the interview be about?
2 Who will be interviewed?
3 What questions do you think the interviewer will ask?

2 You will hear the interview.

a 📼 *10.9* Listen and check your ideas.

b What questions does the interviewer ask?

3 Dr Shamberg uses activities to illustrate his ideas.

a Match the list of ideas and the list of activities.

Ideas	Activities
Pleasure is important for human survival.	going for a walk getting on with each other jumping out of a plane eating
Happy people enjoy the everyday things in life.	chatting with a friend doing a crossword having children
Pleasure means different things to different people.	cooking a meal relaxing in a hot bath

b 📼 *10.9* Listen again and check your answers.

4 Discuss these questions.
1 What do you think of Dr Shamberg's ideas?
2 Should everyone be able to pursue their own 'pleasures'? What about these?
   • taking drugs   • driving fast
   • smoking   • hunting
3 The modern world can offer a very wide range of pleasures. Make a list of some things that were not available a hundred years ago. Have these things improved life or made it worse?

5 Look at the questionnaire about pleasure.

a Choose the ten activities which give you most pleasure. Put them in order 1–10 (1 is the most pleasurable).

b Are there any things that you would like to add to the list?

c Work in a group. Compare your choices. What differences and similarities are there?
   Use these expressions:
   I (don't) like …
   I really enjoy …
   I've never tried …
   I prefer … to …
   I get a lot of pleasure from …

d List the ten things that you spend most of your time doing. How does this list compare to your answers to the questionnaire? Have you got the recipe for a happy life?

6 Make a questionnaire to find out what people hate doing.

a Work in groups, using the questionnaire in **5** as a model. Make a list of about thirty things that you think people dislike doing. (Some may be the same as in the questionnaire!)

b On a separate piece of paper list the ten things that you think will be most unpopular.

c Give your questionnaire to another group and ask them to choose their ten least favourite things. Compare the results to your own predictions.

The pleasure principle

Choose your ten favourite activities and put them in order 1–10.

- playing sports ■
- watching sports ■
- challenging nature
   (eg fishing, rock climbing) ■
- keeping fit ■
- listening to music ■
- relaxing in a hot bath ■
- having a massage ■
- making money ■
- spending money ■
- shopping ■
- going to the cinema/
   watching TV/videos ■
- visiting new places ■
- learning new things ■
- meeting new people ■
- spending time outdoors ■
- watching/playing with animals ■
- redecorating your home ■
- working/studying ■
- meditating ■
- painting ■
- reading a book ■
- playing a musical instrument/
   singing ■
- doing puzzles ■
- daydreaming ■
- being with friends ■
- spending time with your family ■
- playing with children ■
- going to a religious service ■
- helping other people ■
- eating ■
- doing nothing ■

11 The media

Grammar

have to/can: past and future

Grammar in use 1

1 **Imagine you are a politician talking to an audience.**

a Work with a partner. Which of these factors do you think is the most important?
- what you say
- your appearance
- your voice

b Give a percentage for each factor.

c Read the text and check your answers.

2 **Discuss these questions.**

1 How important is image, do you think?
2 Do you agree with Mehrabian's research?
3 Can you think of any examples from your own experience which confirm his research?

Rules

1 **The text uses the verb *have to*.**

a Complete these sentences from the text.
   Obviously film stars _____ right for the part.
   So you _____ too much about content.
   For example, _____ politicians _____ about their appearance?

b Rewrite each sentence in the third person singular.

c How do we make these forms with *have to*?
- a positive statement
- a negative stagement
- a question

➤ Check the rules for *have to* in **Grammar Reference 11.1**.

How important is image? Obviously film stars have to look right for the part, but what about other people in the public eye? For example, do politicians have to think about their appearance, too? Albert Mehrabian studied the effect that speakers have on their audience. His research showed that only 7% of the effect depends on what you say; 38% of the effect comes from your voice; but a huge 55% of the effect comes from your appearance. So you don't have to worry too much about content! Your voice and your appearance are much more important.

Practice

1 What qualities do these people have to have for their jobs?

a Look at the list of possible qualities.

b Work with a partner and complete the table. Can you add any more?

Qualities
be good-looking   be strong   be fit
have a university degree   be young
be married   look honest   be tall
have a nice voice   look attractive

Jobs	has to	doesn't have to
a TV newsreader		
a priest		
a fashion model		
a politician		
a doctor		
a footballer		

2 What do you have to do in your job, or future job?

a Make a list of the things that you have to do and the qualities that you have to have.

b Work with a partner. Ask questions to find out about your partner's job.

EXAMPLES
In your job do you have to work with other people?
Do you have to drive?
What hours do you have to work?

Grammar in use 2

1 🔲 *11.1* **Listen to the interview.**
1 What is Jason Saul's job?
2 What has he recently done?
3 How did he do it?
4 Why won't he be able to do it again?

2 Discuss these questions.
1 How does Jason Saul justify his job?
2 Do you agree with him?
3 Do you think that there should be rules about what newspapers can print?

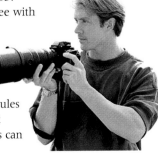

Rules

1 Find examples in tapescript 11.1 to complete the table.

Present	Past	Future	
have to don't have to	_____	_____	(obligation)
can can't	_____	_____	(ability)

2 How do we make questions with *have to* and *can* in the past and future?

➤ Check the rules for *have to* and *can* in **Grammar References 11.1** and **11.2**.

Practice

1 Make an interview with Jason Saul.

a Put the words in the correct order to make questions.
1 the have did photographs you take to?
2 hide did have where to you?
3 see you house clearly could the?
4 long wait did have how you to?
5 photos be to will sell you the able?
6 same you able be the use to will tree?
7 to what you have now will do?
8 lens buy be you to new will able a?

b Work with a partner. Use the questions to roleplay an interview with Jason Saul.

2 Think about your childhood.

a Write down three things that you had to do and three things that you didn't have to do.

EXAMPLES
I had to go to bed at eight o'clock.
I didn't have to go to work.

b Ask other people in the class if their childhood was the same.

EXAMPLE
A What time did you have to go to bed, when you were six?
B I had to go to bed at eight o'clock.
A So did I.

c Could you do these things when you were six?
- read
- swim
- ride a bike
- speak a foreign language
- play computer games
- write

d Compare answers with a partner.

3 Imagine that these things have just happened.

a Think about how your life will change.
What will/won't you have to do?
What will/won't you be able to do?
- You've lost your job.
- You've got married.
- You've retired.
- You've won the national lottery.
- You and your partner have had a baby.
- You've got a place to study abroad.

b Compare answers with a partner, and then with the class.

➤ See **Reflecting on Learning 12**: The verb *to have* p121.

Vocabulary
The media

1 Who are your favourite media people?

a Write the name of your favourite
  - newsreader.
  - TV presenter.
  - DJ.
  - journalist.
  - newspaper.
  - magazine.
  - TV station.
  - TV programme.
  - radio station.
  - film star.
  - film director.
  - TV advertisement.
  - weather presenter.

b Tell your partner about your choices.

2 Match the verbs with the items. Each item can have more than one verb.

switch on switch off listen to watch produce write take record look at read make see	a photograph
	an article
	the TV
	the radio
	a film
	a programme

3 Complete these sentences with *in* or *on*.

1 We were _____ a photograph _____ the newspaper.
2 My dog was _____ an advertisement _____ TV.
3 I've seen that film _____ video. Clint Eastwood's _____ it.
4 I read about it _____ an article _____ a magazine.
5 He was _____ a play _____ the radio.

Reading
Fiona's new look

1 Look at the photographs in the first newspaper article.

a Discuss these questions.
  1 How has the woman's appearance changed?
  2 Which photograph do you prefer and why?

b Read the first two paragraphs and answer the questions.
  1 Who is the woman in the photo?
  2 What is her new job?
  3 What did she do before?
  4 What has she had to change for her new job?

2 Look quickly through the whole text. Match the people and their jobs.

Liz Howell	co-presenter
Michael Wilson	weatherman
John Coleman	image consultant
Frank N Magid	Director of Programmes

3 Read the whole article and answer these questions.
  1 What changes have the image consultants made to Fiona's image?
  2 Why have they made the changes?
  3 Why has Fiona accepted them?

FIONA'S NEW LOOK

Fiona Armstrong has got a new job. The former newsreader from ITN is the co-presenter of GMTV's new breakfast programme.

The breakfast show will start at 6.00 am tomorrow, but Fiona has had to change more than her working hours. The new Fiona has got lighter hair, brighter lipstick and a sexier wardrobe. She will also smile a lot and flirt with the guests on the programme. So why the big change?

The producers want women between 20 and 40 to identify with Fiona, who's 35, and they want people of all ages to find her attractive. So GMTV brought in American image consultant, Frank N Magid to create a whole new image for Fiona. He's known as 'the news doctor' in the States where image consultancy is big business. He decided that Fiona's serious newsreader image had to go. GMTV's Director of Programmes, Liz Howell says 'We want the viewers to fancy the presenters. So we've tried to bring out the nice, friendly side of Fiona and to make her sexier. She now wears brighter colours and shorter skirts. Her jackets are shorter, too, to emphasize her figure. She looks beautiful.'

Fiona's co-presenter, Michael Wilson, has also had to change his image. GMTV want Michael to appeal to women, but they don't want him to alienate male viewers either. Both presenters had to agree to the new image as part of the job.

GMTV start their new breakfast programme tomorrow morning. But not everyone is happy. The news doctors have got it wrong in the past. A few years ago they sacked American weatherman, John Coleman, because he was too dull. After thousands of letters from angry viewers, Coleman was back in his job.

4 **Discuss these questions.**
1 What do you think about the attempt to change Fiona's image?
2 What image do you think they created for Michael Wilson?
3 Do you think Fiona will like her new image?
4 Do you think their new images will be successful?

Language focus:
want someone to …

a Complete this sentence from the text.

GMTV want _____ to women, but they don't want _____ male viewers.

b Use your answers to **3**. What do the programme producers want Fiona to do?

EXAMPLE

They want her to smile a lot.

(inset) as a newsreader

Fiona's new image

5 **What happened to Fiona?**

a Look quickly at this article and answer these questions.
1 Who was it written by?
2 Was it written before or after the other article?
3 What happened? Choose the correct statement.
- ☐ Fiona's new image was a great success.
- ☐ Fiona left the programme.
- ☐ The producers changed Fiona's image again.

b Were your ideas in **4** correct?

HOW MUCH DOES IMAGE MATTER?

Well, I have to say, it was a shock. When I was a newsreader my appearance was never discussed. And I didn't even think about my legs, which were always behind a desk. But when I moved to GMTV my appearance became front page news. Suddenly every newspaper in the country had something to say about my legs, and none of it was very flattering.

I know that image matters. If you're in the public eye you have to look smart and neat. Viewers don't want to see untidy clothes and hair. Image *is* important, but it isn't everything. In all the newspaper articles about the new breakfast programme, nobody mentioned the programme's content or information. They all just criticised my appearance. It was so trivial.

I was unhappy on the new programme right from the start, although I stayed longer than my male co-presenter. We both felt uncomfortable with our artificial images. Then finally I couldn't do it any more, either. I just wasn't being myself and it showed. So I left, too.

I'm starting a new job soon as the presenter of a programme called *Fantastic Facts*, and I feel very good about it. I'll have to look good, of course, but I won't have to wear 'sexy' clothes and smile all the time. I'll be able to choose my own clothes and my own hairstyle. I'll be able to be myself. Then the viewers will be able to concentrate on the content of the programme, not on me.

6 **Read the text more carefully.**

a Answer these questions.
1 What did the newspapers say about Fiona's appearance?
2 Why didn't she like it? (2 reasons)
3 What happened to Fiona's co-presenter?
4 What is Fiona going to do now?
5 Why is she happy about it?

b What do you think about Fiona's ideas? Do you agree?

7 **Write a short summary of the two articles, using this format:**
- Fiona's new job as presenter of GMTV's new breakfast programme
- her new image and the reasons for it
- what happened and why
- what Fiona is going to do now
- how Fiona feels about the whole incident

Listening and speaking
Getting through

1 You will hear Ray Porter making a phone call.

a ▣ *11.2* Listen to the first part and answer these questions.

1 Who is he going to phone?
2 Where does she work?
3 What does he want to phone about?
4 What is the number?

b Tick (✓) the things that happen.

☐ He gets through to the wrong extension.
☐ Kathy is in a meeting.
☐ He calls back.
☐ He hangs up.
☐ He gets through to Kathy's secretary.
☐ The line is engaged.
☐ He dials a wrong number.
☐ Kathy calls him back.
☐ There's no reply.
☐ He leaves a message for Kathy.
☐ Kathy is out.
☐ Kathy is going to be away next week.
☐ He holds on.

2 ▣ *11.2* **Listen to the rest of the conversation and number the events in the correct order.**

Conversation pieces:
Telephone expressions

a Complete the expressions with these words.

moment	hold	wrong	engaged
reply	may	extension	keep	try
message	through	hang	speak

How _____ I help you?

Could I _____ to ...?
Could I have _____ 233, please?
Could I leave a _____ for ...?

I'm sorry, the line's _____ .
There's no _____ .
I think you've got the _____ extension.
Would you like to _____ ?

I'll _____ on.
I'll _____ again later.

I'm sorry to _____ you.

Just one _____ , please.
I'm just putting you _____ now.

b Look at tapescript 11.2 and check your answers.

c Practise the conversations with a partner, using the tapescript.

3 **Work with a partner. Take it in turns to be the caller. Make conversations for these situations.**

1 You telephone Arthur Border (extension 5674) to change your meeting next week from Monday to Tuesday. His line is engaged. You leave a message with his secretary.

2 You telephone Doctor Sabatini (extension 874). There is no reply. You ask to leave a message with her secretary, asking her to call you back before 4.00.

3 You telephone Pieter Jensen (extension 1276). His line is engaged. You hold on. You finally get through. Tell him that your plane is late, but you should be there by 3.30.

4 You telephone Celia Appleby (01789 564382), but you get the wrong number.

'Hello, this is air traffic control. Please leave your message after the bleep and we'll…'

'Actually, Madam, I don't know how you managed it, but you **are** speaking to somebody in authority.'

Pronunciation
Clusters; list intonation

1 Consonant clusters

English words often have more than one consonant sound together. We call these consonant clusters. You normally have to pronounce all of the consonants. This is very important when the cluster is at the end of the word and carries part of the meaning, such as a past tense or a plural.

EXAMPLES
changed /tʃeɪndʒd/
fields /fiːldz/

Consonant clusters can also occur at the beginning or in the middle of a word.

EXAMPLES
strong /strɒŋ/
newsreader /ˈnjuːzriːdə/

a Say these words.

lip**stick**	ward**robe**	**emph**a**s**ized	com**pete**
aga**inst**	**str**aight	sub**jects**	shoul**dn't**
pu**bl**ic	cho**pped**	sho**cked**	wa**nts**

b ▭ *11.3* Listen, check and repeat.

2 List intonation

When we say a list of things, the intonation rises on each item in the list and then falls on the last item.

a ▭ *11.4* Listen to this sentence.

They changed her clothes, her hairstyle and her make-up.

b Mark the intonation, then say these sentences.

1 Footballers have to be young, strong and very fit.

2 Mehrabian studied the effects of appearance, voice and content.

3 We get our news from TV, radio and newspapers.

4 I want you to relax, be friendly and smile.

5 For this recipe you need potatoes, beans, tomatoes and oil.

c ▭ *11.5* Listen, check and repeat.

Extension: Reading and listening
Gladiators!

1 Look at the photographs. They are from a TV programme.

a Discuss these questions.
1. What do you think the progamme is about?
2. Who are the people in the pictures?
3. What do you think the people have to do?

b Read the text and check your ideas.

c Discuss these questions.
1. Is there a similar TV programme in your country?
2. The programme is described as 'a gruelling competition'. What do you think *gruelling* means?
3. Why do you think people want to be contenders?
4. Would you like to try this game?

GLADIATORS!

They're big. They're strong. They're tough. They're also the stars of one of the most popular programmes on TV at the moment. They are the Gladiators. At 5.40 every Saturday evening millions of viewers of all ages switch on. For the next hour they watch four brave contenders – two men and two women – take part in TV's most gruelling competition.

In each programme the contenders have to compete against the Gladiators in six different events. If they win they score points. If they lose they just get the bruises. The final event is the Eliminator. The Gladiators take a rest here, because the contenders compete against each other. They have to race over obstacles, such as nets, ladders and ropes. It's a most gruelling end to a gruelling competition. But it's great TV!

2 **Read the text again. Mark these sentences *True* (✓) or *False* (✓).**

1 *Gladiators* is the most popular programme on TV. ☐
2 Only young people like the programme. ☐
3 The programme is on at 5.40 every evening. ☐
4 The programme lasts for an hour. ☐
5 All the contenders are men. ☐
6 There are six events in each programme. ☐
7 The Gladiators don't take part in the Eliminator. ☐
8 The Eliminator is the easiest event. ☐

3 **Look at the photographs of some of the events.**

a Label the photographs with these words.

platform	ring	wall	stick	rope

b Now look at the three events on this page. Describe what you think the contenders and Gladiators have to do in each event, using the photographs and these verbs.

swing across	hang on	pull off	climb up
get to	knock off	catch	chase

4 **You will hear three contenders talking about their experiences on *Gladiators*.**

a ▣ *11.6* Listen and complete the table. Use these names to help you.

Events		Gladiators		
Danger Zone	Duel	Saracen	Scorpio	Jet
the Wall	Hang Tough	Warrior	Trojan	Hawk

	Event	Gladiator	Result
Contender 1			
Contender 2			
Contender 3			

b ▣ *11.6* Listen again. What did each contender have to do?

c Compare the descriptions of the events to your own ideas from **3**.

d If you had to try an event, which one would you choose and why?

5 **Devise another event for *Gladiators*.**

a Work in groups and decide
• what the equipment is.
• what the contenders have to do.
• what the Gladiators have to do.
• how the contenders score.

b Draw a plan of the event.

c Describe your event to the class.

12 Planet Earth

Grammar
The passive

Grammar in use

1 Look at the cartoon.

a What do you think the text will be about?

b Can you identify any of these things on these pages?

> rubbish   debris   space   satellite   spacecraft   orbit   rocket

c Read the text and check your ideas.

2 Answer these questions.
1 What is it about?
2 How has the situation been created?
3 Why is the situation dangerous?
4 What will happen in the future?

The rubbish dump in the sky

On 4 October 1957 the first satellite, *Sputnik*, was launched. Since then, thousands of spacecraft have been sent into space. Every few weeks new satellites are put into orbit. Unfortunately, space is being polluted by debris from these space flights. More than 70,000 objects have been left in space. Parts of rockets have been left. Old satellites have been abandoned. Other items, including a glove, a spanner and a camera, have been lost by astronauts. The situation up there is becoming dangerous. Both Russian and American spacecraft have been damaged. An astronaut would be killed if he or she was hit by a piece of rubbish. It would cost billions of dollars to collect all the debris, but if nothing is done the situation will only get worse. Sooner or later a satellite will be destroyed by a large piece of rubbish and thousands more pieces of debris will be scattered.

3 What do you think should be done about the situation in the text?

Rules

1 The text shows many verbs in the passive.

a Complete these sentences from the text.

1 *On 4 October 1957 the first satellite, Sputnik, _____ .*
2 *Since then, thousands of spacecraft _____ into space.*
3 *Every few weeks new satellites _____ into orbit.*
4 *Unfortunately, space _____ _____ by debris from these space flights.*
5 *An astronaut _____ if he or she was hit by a piece of rubbish.*
6 *Sooner or later a satellite _____ _____ by a large piece of rubbish.*

b The verbs in the sentences are all in the passive.
1 What two parts does a passive verb have?
2 What tense is each sentence in?
3 Which part of the passive verb changes to show the tense?

c Complete the rule.

> We form the passive with the correct tense of the verb _____ + the past participle.

d Find more examples of the passive in the text. Which tense are they in?

2 When do we use the passive?

a Look at these two sentences. Do they mean the same?
Russia launched the first satellite in 1957.
(ACTIVE)
The first satellite was launched by Russia in 1957.
(PASSIVE)

b Answer these questions.
1 If we remove *Russia* from the active sentence, we get *Launched the first satellite in 1957.* Does it still make sense?

2 If we remove *by Russia* from the passive sentence, we get *The first satellite was launched in 1957.* Does it still make sense?

c Complete the rule with *more* or *less*.

> We use the passive when the action is _____ important than who or what does the action (the agent).

d Often we don't even know the agent. Look again at the sentences in **Rules 1**, and find examples with no agent.

e Sometimes we do know the agent. Find examples in the sentences in **Rules 1**. How is the agent shown?

➤ Check the rules for the passive in **Grammar Reference 12.1**.

Practice

1 Put the verbs in brackets into the present simple passive.

Putting a satellite into orbit.

1 The satellite _____ (build).
2 It _____ (test).
3 The satellite _____ (take) to the rocket launch site.
4 The rocket _____ (prepare).
5 The rocket and satellite _____ (launch).
6 The lower parts of the rocket _____ (dump).
7 The satellite _____ (put) into orbit.
8 The satellite's own rockets _____ (fire).
9 The satellite _____ (move) into the correct orbit.
10 The rest of the rocket _____ (leave) in space.

2 Look at this text about *Skylab*.

a Complete the text with these verbs in the past simple passive.

destroy
sell
hurt
scatter
send
abandon
hit
find
launch

> In 1973 a 75-tonne space station called *Skylab* _____ by the USA. Three crews of three astronauts _____ to *Skylab*, but at the end of 1974, it _____ . *Skylab* stayed in space until 1979. Then it fell out of its orbit and headed towards the Earth. A lot of the space station burnt up when it entered the atmosphere. But not all of it _____ . Large pieces _____ across the Indian Ocean. Australia _____ by some fragments. Fortunately nobody _____ . A lot of the pieces _____ by Australian farmers. The pieces _____ for very high prices.

b 🔊 *12.1* Listen and check.

3 Change these sentences from the active into the passive, keeping the same tense.
1 The American astronaut, Michael Collins, dropped a camera.
2 Eventually a piece of debris will hit an astronaut.
3 A normal space suit would not protect the astronaut.
4 Rubbish is damaging communications satellites.
5 Today's satellites will create more rubbish.
6 A piece of debris cracked one of the space shuttle's windows.
7 The space shuttle has brought some satellites back to Earth.
8 Scientists found 186 marks on one satellite.
9 Space debris caused 166 of the marks.

4 Rubbish is a problem on Earth, too. Discuss these questions.
1 Why is so much rubbish produced?
2 What is done with today's rubbish?
3 What effects is this having?
4 How will the situation change in the future?

Vocabulary
The natural world

1 Do you normally associate these words with space or with the Earth?

a Write S or E next to each one.

planet	North Pole	continent
moon	desert	island
peninsula	coast	lake
volcano	earthquake	atmosphere
star	ocean	sea
mountain	sun	satellite
river	equator	solar system
hemisphere	comet	orbit

b Look at the picture. Label as many of the things as possible, using the words in the box.

Reading
Comet!

1 Read the first two paragraphs and the last paragraph of the text. Each paragraph describes a similar event.

a Answer these questions.
  1 What are the three events?
  2 When do, or did, they happen?

b What results do you think the imaginary event in the second paragraph will have?

2 Read the whole text quickly and answer the questions.
  1 Which of the places on the map are mentioned?
  2 How many fragments of the comet hit the Earth?
  3 Where do they land? Mark the places on the map.

3 **Read paragraphs 3–5 more carefully.**

a Match the items in column A and column B.

A	B
First fragment	shock waves
Second fragment	clouds of dust and water vapour
Effect	tidal wave

b Look at the events in column B.
   What causes each one?
   What effects does each have?

c Use the information above and write sentences to summarize paragraphs 3–5.

4 **Read the final paragraph and discuss these questions.**

1 What evidence is given that the events of 2094 could really happen?
2 How do you feel about the possibility?
3 What could be done to prevent it?

5 **Imagine it is two weeks before the fragments of the comet hit the Earth. There are plans to send missiles into space to destroy the fragments.**

a Work with a partner. One of you is a reporter and one is an astronomer. Ask and answer questions about
   • what is going to happen.
   • the plans to destroy the fragments.
   • what will happen if the plan fails.

b Compare your ideas with the class.

6 **Imagine another disaster, such as a storm, an earthquake or a volcanic eruption.**

   Write a newspaper report about it, using this format:

   Paragraph 1 Describe the scene at the moment.
   Paragraph 2 Describe what happened.
   Paragraph 3 Describe the actual and probable effects.

In July 1994 Jupiter, the largest planet in our solar system, was struck by 21 pieces of a comet. When the fragments landed in the southern hemisphere of the giant planet, the explosions were watched by astronomers here on Earth. But what if our own planet was hit by a comet?

The year is 2094. It has been announced that a comet is heading towards the Earth. Most of it will miss our planet, but two fragments will probably hit the southern hemisphere. The news has caused panic. Stock markets around the world have been thrown into chaos.

On 17 July, a fragment four kilometres wide enters the Earth's atmosphere with a massive explosion. About half of the fragment is destroyed and pieces are scattered through the atmosphere. But the core survives and hits the South Atlantic at 200 times the speed of sound. The sea boils and a huge hole is made in the sea bed. An enormous tidal wave is created and spreads outwards from the hole. The wall of water, a kilometre high, rushes towards southern Africa at 800 kilometres an hour. Cities on the African coast are totally destroyed and millions of people are drowned. The wave moves into the Indian Ocean and heads towards Asia. Coastal cities are evacuated and thousands are killed in the panic.

Before the wave reaches South America, the second fragment of the comet lands in Argentina. Earthquakes and volcanoes are set off in the Andes mountains. The shock waves move north into California and all around the Pacific Ocean. The cities of Los Angeles, San Francisco and Tokyo are completely destroyed by earthquakes.

Millions of people are already dead south of the equator, but the north won't escape for long. Tons of debris are thrown into the atmosphere by the explosions and the volcanoes. As the sun is hidden by clouds of dust and water vapour, temperatures around the world fall to almost zero. Crops are ruined. The sun won't be seen again for many years. Wars break out as countries fight for food. A year later civilization has collapsed. No more than 10 million people have survived.

Could it really happen? In fact, it has already happened more than once in the history of the Earth. The dinosaurs were on the Earth for over 160 million years. Then 65 million years ago they suddenly disappeared. Many scientists believe that the Earth was hit by a piece of space debris. The dinosaurs couldn't survive in the cold climate that followed and they became extinct. Will we meet the same end?

Listening and speaking
Oh, really?

1 Match the sentences and photographs. How would you respond to the news?

1 Peter and I are getting married.
2 I've got an interview for a job today.
3 John can't play today. It seems he's had an accident.
4 Did you know Tony and Rosie have split up?
5 I won the gold medal in the race.
6 I'm expecting a baby.
7 I'm afraid I failed my driving test.
8 Have you heard? Sue had her baby on Saturday.
9 Happy Birthday, Mummy!

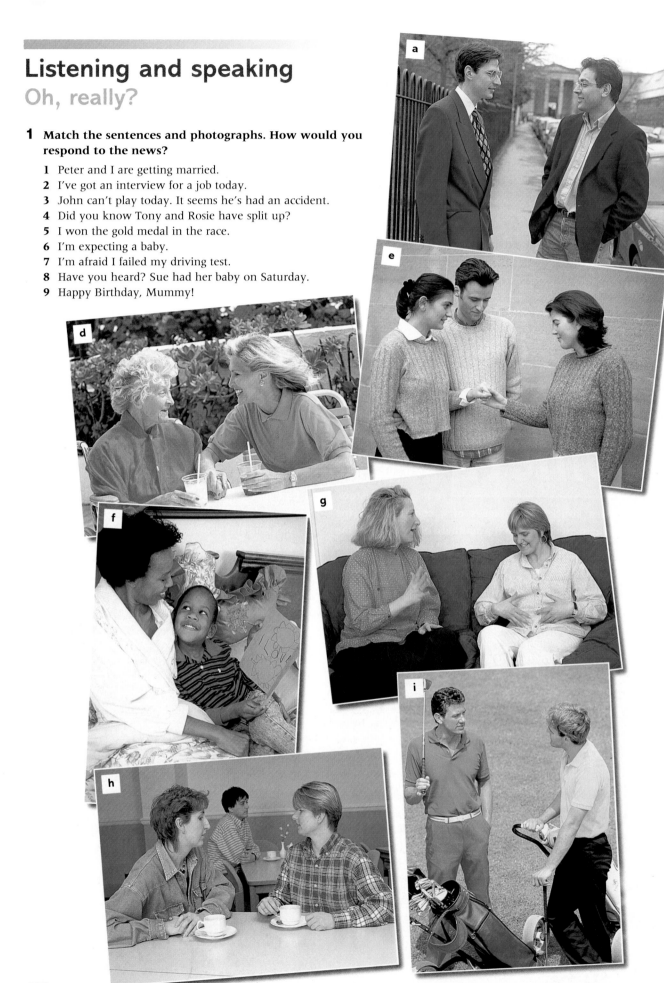

2 Look at these responses.

a Choose the most appropriate response for each of the sentences in **1**.

Oh, really? When did that happen?
Thank you very much. How sweet of you.
That's wonderful news! When's it due?
Congratulations! When's the happy day?
And a Merry Christmas to you, too.
Oh dear. It's nothing serious, I hope.
It's just what I've always wanted.
Oh wonderful! Was it a boy or a girl?
Cheers! All the best!
That's all right. Don't mention it.
Well done! I knew you could do it.
Happy Anniversary!
Oh well, never mind. Better luck next time!
Good luck! I'll keep my fingers crossed for you.

b 📟 *12.2* Listen and check.

c Some of the responses are not appropriate for the sentences in **1**. When would you use them?

3 📟 *12.2* Listen again and pay attention to the intonation.

a Practise saying the responses.

b Work with a partner and roleplay the conversations.

c Choose two of the conversations and continue them.

4 Make more conversations.

a Look at these situations.
- You've just passed your driving test.
- A member of your family is in hospital.
- You've just won a free holiday in a competition.
- You've just lost your job.
- A friend of yours is getting married.
- You're going to study abroad for two years.
- It's your friend's birthday. You've got a present for him/her.

b Work with a partner and make the conversations.

c Choose one of the conversations and roleplay it in front of the class.

Pronunciation
/ə/; word linking (1)

1 The /ə/ sound

Many words in English contain the /ə/ (schwa) sound. A syllable with this sound is always unstressed.

a Look at this list of words. Circle the syllables with the /ə/ sound. Not all of the words contain the sound.

satellite	probably
volcano	explosion
camera	dinosaur
rubbish	disappear
unfortunately	survive
spanner	collapse
atmosphere	million
accident	extinct
yesterday	evacuate
astronomer	suddenly

b 📟 *12.3* Listen and check your ideas.

c 📟 *12.3* Listen again and repeat.

2 Word linking (1)

When we speak, we run words together. Here is one way in which we do this.
When there is a consonant sound at the end of one word and the next word starts with a vowel, we run the final consonant on to the vowel.

She was eighteen years old.

He had a gold earring.

a Mark the word linking in these sentences.

1 He's had an accident.

2 My birthday's in August.

3 It landed in the South Atlantic.

4 Their plane arrives at eleven.

5 John and Ellen have split up.

6 It's what I've always wanted.

7 I'm expecting a baby.

8 I get up at eight o'clock.

b 📟 *12.4* Listen and check.

c 📟 *12.4* Listen again and repeat.

Extension: Reading and listening
Going for gold

1 Look at the title and pictures.

a What words would you expect to find in an article on this topic? Make a list.

b Underline the topic words in the article and compare them to your list. Add any new words.

2 Each paragraph has a sentence missing.

a Read the article carefully and write the number of each sentence in the correct place.
   1 About 83% of it is used for jewellery.
   2 Sailors, for example, used to wear a gold earring.
   3 People have always been fascinated by gold.
   4 The word *carat* comes from the Greek word, *keration*, which means a carob seed.
   5 When gold is bought and sold, it isn't usually moved.

b Explain how you decided where the sentences belong.

c 📼 *12.5* Listen to the complete text and check your answers.

3 Mark these sentences *True (✓)* or *False (✗)*.
   1 Twenty-four carat gold is the most expensive. ☐
   2 Gold is weighed with carob seeds. ☐
   3 Most gold is made into jewellery. ☐
   4 Gold is found in Australia. ☐
   5 All the gold in Fort Knox is owned by the American government. ☐
   6 The first gold coins were produced over 3,000 years ago. ☐
   7 Military pilots wear gold earrings. ☐
   8 The Pharaohs were buried in the Pyramids. ☐
   9 Eldorado was destroyed for gold. ☐
  10 Gold was discovered in California in 1849. ☐

4 Discuss these questions.
   1 Why is gold usually mixed with other metals?
   2 Why is gold used for teeth?
   3 Why is gold bought by governments and individuals?
   4 Why isn't gold usually moved from bank to bank?
   5 Gold is used as a symbol of value. It also has some practical uses. How is it used in your country?

5 The importance of gold is often shown in expressions.

a Here are some English examples. What do you think they mean?

   This is a golden opportunity.
   Silence is golden.
   He's been as good as gold.
   She's worth her weight in gold.
   We've struck gold this time.

b What expressions do you have in your language that use the word *gold*? Translate them into English.

6 Are their any legends or stories about gold in your country's history? Tell the class.

Pure gold is rare. It has been used for over 6,000 years, but there are still only about 110,000 tons in the world. It is usually mixed with other metals. The proportion of gold is shown in carats. Pure gold is twenty-four carat and the cheapest is nine carat. These seeds were used to weigh gold and diamonds.

Most gold today is found in South Africa (612 tons a year) and North America (459 tons a year). Of the rest about 9% is used by industry, about 6% is used for coins and 2% is made into gold teeth. Gold is usually found in very small pieces or 'nuggets'. The largest nugget, the Holtermann Nugget, was found in 1872 in Australia. It weighed 214 kilograms.

The largest reserves of gold are held in the USA in the Federal Reserve Bank and Fort Knox. The second biggest stores are held by the Bank of England and the Bank of France. Not all of this gold belongs to the governments of these countries. A lot of it is owned by companies, other governments, and individuals. Only the names on a piece of paper are changed. The gold itself stays in the bank.

The first gold coins were used in Turkey in 670 BC. But gold has always been accepted as money anywhere in the world. If they were shipwrecked, they could pay to get home again. Gold is still given to military pilots for the same reason.

How many crimes have been committed and how many lives have been lost for it? The gold of the Pharaohs was stolen from their tombs in the Pyramids. The Inca and Aztec empires were destroyed for gold.

Hundreds of men died in the jungles of South America as they searched for the golden city of Eldorado. In 1849 thousands of people left their homes to join the California Gold Rush. Many were killed by Indians, outlaws and disease.

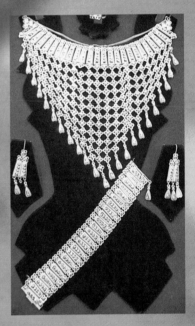

13 Time

Grammar
The past perfect tense

Grammar in use

1 Look at the headline and photographs.

a Discuss these questions.

  1 What does *amnesia* mean?

  2 What is the connection between the photographs?

  3 What do you think happened to the people?

b Read the article and check your ideas.

2 Discuss these questions.

  1 How has the world changed since 1973?

  2 What problems do you think Sarah's amnesia caused for

    • Sarah?

    • her family?

The forgotten years

It was 1973 and Sarah Simms was a happy 19-year-old. She had a nice job in a film laboratory, and in the evenings she went out with her boyfriend. She loved dancing, especially to her favourite pop group, T. Rex.

Then she woke up in a hospital bed. A man was talking to her. He said that he was her husband, but she didn't recognize him. In fact, she didn't like him very much. She thought he looked very old. Some other visitors were standing around her bed, too. She didn't recognize any of them except her sister, Sally, and even she looked twenty years older. But that's because Sally *was* twenty years older, and so was Sarah.

Two days earlier Sarah had been in a car crash. The accident had erased twenty years of her memory. It was now 1993, but for Sarah it was 1973 and she was still a teenager. She'd forgotten the twenty years in between.

In those twenty years Sarah had got married. (In 1973 she hadn't met her husband.) And she'd had two children – Alexander, 11, and Linda, 9. The world had also changed dramatically. What, for example, was a word processor, a microwave or a compact disc? Those things had not been invented in 1973. Had Britain really had a woman prime minister? And *where* had all her favourite pop stars gone?

Doctors say that Sarah's amnesia is rare, but they hope that her memory will slowly return. Her husband Michael hopes so, too. 'Life has been difficult since the accident,' he says. 'Things have changed a lot. It's hard when a wife and mother thinks she's still a teenager.'

Sarah and her husband Michael in 1993.

Sarah and Michael in 1974, two years before their marriage.

Rules

1 The text uses the past perfect tense.

a Complete these sentences from the text.

The accident _____ twenty years of her memory.

She _____ the twenty years in between.

In 1973 she _____ her husband.

Those things _____ in 1973.

b How do we form the past perfect tense? Complete the rules.

> We make positive statements with
>
> _____ (short form: _____) + _____
>
> We make negative statements with
>
> _____ (short form: _____) + _____

c Find more examples of the past perfect tense in the story.

d Look at the two questions. How do we make questions in the past perfect tense?

2 When do we use the past perfect tense?

a Look at this sentence.

Sarah didn't recognize her husband, because she had lost her memory.

The sentence describes two events:

Sarah didn't recognize her husband.
Sarah lost her memory.

b Answer these questions.
1 Which event happened first?
2 Which tense is used for each event?

c Complete the rule with *before* or *after*.

> The past perfect tense describes events that
> happened _____ an event in the past tense.

➤ Check the rules for the past perfect tense in **Grammar Reference 13.1**.

Practice

1 Look at this list.

a Say whether these things had or hadn't happened to Sarah in 1973.

> | | |
> |---|---|
> | start work | have a favourite pop |
> | see the Beatles | group |
> | use a personal computer | hair/ turn grey |
> | finish school | have a boyfriend |
> | hear of Margaret Thatcher | leave home |
> | be abroad | |

b 🔊 *13.1* Listen to Sarah and check your answers.

2 Complete these sentences. Put the verbs in brackets into the past tense or the past perfect tense.

1 Sarah _____(not recognize) her husband, because in 1973 she _____(not meet) him.

2 Her hair _____(turn) grey and she _____(not like) that.

3 She _____(not know) how to use a microwave oven, because they _____(not be invented) in 1973.

4 She _____(cry) when she found out that her father _____(die).

5 Clothes _____(look) very strange, because fashions _____(change) a lot.

6 She _____(not know) that the Cold War _____(end).

7 TV programmes _____(become) more violent, so she _____(not want) to watch them.

8 She _____(feel) sad, because the singer of T. Rex _____(be killed) in a car crash.

3 Think of a point in your life when your life changed.

EXAMPLES
- *you became a teenager*
- *you were eighteen*
- *you started/left school*
- *you got married*
- *1990*

a Write down
- four things that you hadn't done before then.
- four things that you had done before then.

b Tell your partner, and answer any questions that your partner asks.

EXAMPLE

Before I was eighteen, I hadn't been to college, and I hadn't lived on my own. I had always lived with my family …

Vocabulary
Time expressions

1 Put these words in the correct order from the shortest to the longest.

season	hour	century	second	year
day	minute	decade	month	week

2 Write down
- the days of the week.
- the months of the year.
- the four seasons.

3 We say years like this:

1973 *nineteen seventy-three*
1600 *sixteen hundred*
1502 *fifteen oh two*

a Work with a partner. Practise saying these years.

1772 1912 1066 1909 1800 1980 1812 1700 1802

b Write down some more years. Dictate them to your partner.

4 Which prepositions do we use with time expressions?

a Put these words and phrases in the correct columns.

the weekend   tomorrow afternoon   ten o'clock   Easter
two days ago   my birthday   Tuesday   the afternoon
7.15   Wednesday morning   1922   Wednesday 9 May
tonight   the seventeenth century   next week   last year
this evening   Christmas Day   yesterday   midnight
September   night   10 January   the 1960s   summer

in	on	at	no preposition

b Which kinds of time expressions are used with *in, on* and *at*? Write down your ideas.

➤ Check in **Grammar Reference 13.2**.

5 Ask and answer these questions.
1 Which year were you born in?
2 When's your birthday?
3 What time do you usually get up?
4 When do you normally go on holiday?
5 When did you last go to the cinema?
6 When did you last write a letter?
7 When did you last make a phone call?
8 When are you going to the hairdresser's?

Reading
Body clock

1 Look at the pictures and the title of the article.

a Discuss these questions.
1 What is the woman doing in the photograph?
2 What do you think she has done?
3 Why did she do it?

b Read the first two paragraphs and check your ideas.

2 What do you think the results of the experiment were?

a Work in groups and consider these things:
- sleeping
- emotions
- eating
- sense of time

b Read the rest of the article and check your ideas.

3 Look at this list with a partner.

a Which things did she have in the cave? Why did or didn't she have them?

a tape recorder   a dog   a clock
a CD player   an English course   food
playing cards   a computer   books
two mice   a window   a telephone
a watch   lights   a television   a radio

b Read the article again and check your ideas.

4 Answer these questions.
1 What happened to Stefania's body rhythms?
2 What did the experiment show?
3 In what way do individual body clocks vary?

5 Discuss these questions.
1 Would you like to do what Stefania did? Why/why not?
2 If you did, how would you spend your time? What would you like/miss most?
3 What patterns does your body clock work to? (e.g. When do you naturally wake up/eat/feel at your best?)
4 What external and internal stimuli determine these patterns?
5 Do your patterns differ from those of other people that you live with? What problems does this cause?

Language focus: Nouns used as adjectives

a Find expressions in the text that mean the same as these:
Stefania is a decorator and she's 27 years old.
Her day underground was not 24 hours long.

b What do you notice about the words *years* and *hours* in the expressions?

c What would you call these things?
1 a man who is 67 years old
2 a working day that lasts eight hours
3 a programme that lasts 30 minutes
4 a computer that costs 590 dollars
5 a bag that weighs three pounds
6 a bottle that holds two litres

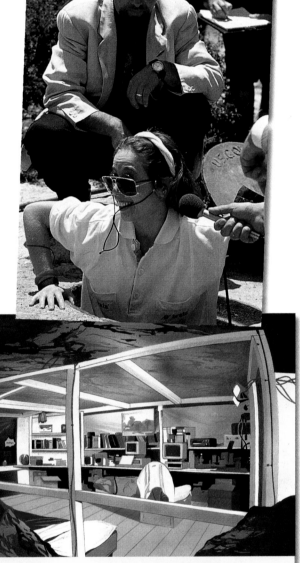

BODY CLOCK

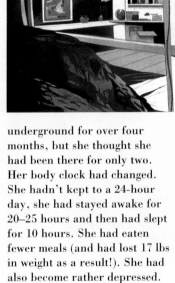

On May 23 1989 Stefania Follini emerged from a cave at Carlsbad, New Mexico. She hadn't seen the sun for eighteen and a half weeks. Stefania was a volunteer in an Italian research programme, and the scientists in the programme were studying body rhythms. In this experiment Stefania, a 27-year-old decorator, had spent 130 days in a cave 30 feet underground.

During her time in the cave, Stefania had been completely alone except for two white mice. Her living quarters had been very comfortable, but there had been nothing to tell her the time. She'd had no clocks or watches, no television or radio. There had been no natural light and the temperature had been kept at a constant 21 degrees Celsius.

The results were very interesting. Stefania had been underground for over four months, but she thought she had been there for only two. Her body clock had changed. She hadn't kept to a 24-hour day, she had stayed awake for 20–25 hours and then had slept for 10 hours. She had eaten fewer meals (and had lost 17 lbs in weight as a result!). She had also become rather depressed.

How had she spent her time in the cave? As part of the experiment she'd done some physical and mental tests. She'd recorded her daily activities and the results of the tests on a computer. (This computer had been her only link to the outside world.) For entertainment she'd played cards, read books and listened to music. She'd also learnt English from tapes.

The experiment showed that our body clocks are affected by light and temperature. For example, the pattern of day and night makes us wake up and go to sleep. However, people are affected in different ways. Some people wake up naturally at 5.00 am, but others don't start to wake up till 9.00 or 10.00 am. This affects the whole daily rhythm. As a result the early risers are at their best in the late morning. The late risers, on the other hand, are tired during the day and only come to life in the afternoon or evening!

Listening and speaking
Arranging a time

1 **We write and say dates in different ways.**

a How do we say these dates?

EXAMPLE

22/11   **the** *twenty-second* **of** *November*
November **the** *twenty-second*

30/1	4/7	22/4	2/5	1/8	23/9
12/11	5/12	18/3	3/6	21/2	26/10

b What were important dates for you in the past year? Tell a partner about them, and answer any questions that your partner asks.

EXAMPLES

- *your birthday*
- *your wedding anniversary*
- *birthdays of other members of the family*
- *a national holiday*
- *your summer holiday*

2 **You will hear three conversations.**

a Look at the photographs. What do you think is happening in each one?

b 🔲 *13.2* Listen and check your ideas.

c 🔲 *13.2* Listen again and write down
- the dates mentioned.
- the dates accepted.

d In the conversations you hear all the months of the year except three. Which three?

➤ See **Grammar Reference 13.3**.

Conversation pieces: Arranging a time

a Look at these expressions from the conversations.

Could you give me some information about …?
Could I make an appointment with …?
Can I change my appointment on … to …?

I want to leave on … and return on …
Have you got any seats available on …?

I'm afraid … is fully booked.
There's a flight at/on …
We have some seats available on …
I'm afraid there's nothing left in/till …
Can you come on …?

b Who would say each expression?

c Reconstruct the conversations with a partner. Use the expressions above and your answers to **2**.

d Look at tapescript 13.2 and check your answers.

3 With your partner make new conversations with this information.

1 **A** Ask for flight times to Toronto. Give dates.
  B Give times.
  A Accept one of the times.

2 **A** Phone to make an appointment with Dr Clark.
  B Offer a time and date.
  A You can't make that. Ask for an alternative.
  B Offer two alternative dates.
  A Accept one date.

3 **A** You booked some tickets for a show, but you want to change them. Give the date.
  B Offer two alternative dates.
  A Choose one alternative.

4 **A** You want to arrange a meeting with a colleague. Suggest a date.
  B You can't make it. Suggest a later date.
  A That's no good for you. You're going abroad then. Give the dates.
  B Suggest a new date.
  A Accept.

There's a message coming through – it says,
'Sorry, he's at a meeting'.

Pronunciation
-u-; word linking (2)

1 The vowel -u-

We usually pronounce the vowel -u- with one of three sounds.

a 🔲 *13.3* Look at the table and listen to the examples.

/ʌ/	/ʊ/	/juː/
much	*put*	*computer*

b Write these words in the correct column.

> bus full museum sun study during cut
> under music push up pull brush huge
> bush university use tune just bull pub

c 🔲 *13.4* Listen and check your ideas.
d 🔲 *13.4* Listen again and repeat.

2 Word linking (2)

In Unit 12 we saw that we run a final consonant sound onto a word beginning with a vowel. Some words have a silent consonant at the end, especially words ending in -r, -w, and -y.

EXAMPLES
car /kɑː(r)/   *few* /fjuː(w)/   *my* /maɪ(j)/

When one of these words comes before a vowel, we pronounce the consonant that is normally silent and run it on.

EXAMPLES
My car is blue.   /maɪkɑːrɪzbluː/
a few apples   /əfjuːwæplz/
my arm   /maɪjɑːm/

a Where will the extra consonant be pronounced in these sentences?

1 She slept for eight hours.
2 How old are you?
3 We spent our holiday in Spain.
4 This is our own house.
5 Go and play outside.
6 Now it's my turn.
7 It's at the other end.
8 He's my uncle.

b 🔲 *13.5* Listen and check.

c 🔲 *13.5* Listen again and repeat.

Extension: Reading and listening
The strange story of Martin Guerre

1 **The paragraphs below tell the first part of the true story of Martin Guerre.**

a Look quickly at the paragraphs and answer these questions.
  1 When did the story take place?
  2 Where did it happen?
  3 Who are these people?

  - Martin
  - Sangxi
  - Bertrande
  - Pierre

b The paragraphs are in the wrong order. Number them in the correct order.

2 🔲 *13.6* **Listen to the first part of the story and check your order.**

3 **Answer these questions.**
  1 Why did Martin and Bertrande get married?
  2 Why did Martin leave the village?
  3 How long was he away?
  4 Why did some people believe that Martin was not the real Martin?
  5 Why did Pierre go to court?
  6 What was the result of the trial?

4 **Discuss these questions.**
  1 What do you think Martin did while he was away?
  2 Do you think this new Martin was the same Martin that had left the village?
  3 What do you think happened in the end?

5 🔲 *13.7* **Listen. You will hear the end of the story.**

a Tick (✓) the things you hear.

  ☐ man with a wooden leg
  ☐ blind woman
  ☐ wounded
  ☐ fallen in love
  ☐ Arnaud du Tilh
  ☐ murdered
  ☐ doctor
  ☐ soldier
  ☐ similar
  ☐ Italy
  ☐ hanged

b How did the story end?

6 **Imagine you are Martin or Bertrande. After the trial you sell your story to a newspaper. Write the story.**

strange story of Martin Guerre

☐ The marriage was not a happy one. Martin was a tall and strong young man, but he was lazy and bad-tempered, and he treated Bertrande very badly. Martin had half of the family's farm. Sangxi's brother, Pierre, had the other half. But while Pierre worked hard on his part of the farm, Martin spent all his time with his friends in the village.

☐ Then one day Pierre received some strange information. Someone said that he had seen Martin Guerre in Flanders. The village shoemaker was also sure that Martin's shoes were now three sizes smaller than before he had left. This was Pierre's chance. He went to court and claimed that this new Martin was not the real Martin Guerre.

1️⃣ It was 1538 and in the village of Artigat in south-west France there was a wedding. The bride was Bertrande de Rols and the bridegroom was Martin Guerre. They didn't love each other. The marriage had been arranged by Martin's father, Sangxi, in order to unite the two richest families in the village.

☐ At the trial some people (including Martin's four sisters) said that the new Martin was the real Martin, but other people said that he wasn't. Finally, the judge decided that he really was Martin. But that was not the end of the story.

☐ Then eight years later, Martin suddenly returned. He had changed a lot while he had been away. In fact, he was like a new man. He was pleasant and helpful, and treated Bertrande well. He also worked hard on the farm. Bertrande and Martin now lived happily together and they soon had a daughter.

☐ Their happy life did not last long, however. While Martin had been away, Sangxi had died, and because Martin had disappeared, Pierre had inherited everything. Now that Martin had returned, Pierre would have to give him half of the inheritance – £7,000. Pierre and Martin argued about the money for three years.

☐ One day Sangxi caught his son in the barn. He was stealing some of Pierre's produce. Sangxi was furious, so the next day Martin secretly left the village. The family waited for news, but none came. Martin Guerre had simply disappeared. Only Sangxi knew why.

14 Work

Grammar
Tense revision

1 Do you think you are efficient or do you waste time?

a Read the text and answer these questions.
1 What is the text about?
2 Who is Sam Flowers?
3 What is the result of wasting time?
4 What do you do with a time log?
5 Why do people use them?

b Think about your own life. Do you agree with Sam Flowers?

2 Imagine a typical day in your life.

a Make a time log for it. (See **3b** for an example.)

b Discuss your time log with a partner. What differences and similarities are there?

3 Where did the morning go?

a Look at the photographs. What is Kate doing in each one?

MANAGING YOUR TIME

'Wasting time is like wasting money.' This is the slogan of Time Management Systems.

'Most people,' says Sam Flowers of TMS, 'waste too much time on doing trivial things like finding telephone numbers, looking for pieces of paper on their desks, and walking from one part of a building to another. These can waste hours of your day. Then you haven't got time for the important things. This applies to both your professional and your personal life.'

The first step towards managing your time better is keeping a time log. In a time log you record everything that you do during the day. Then you calculate how much time you spent on each thing – travelling, telephoning, eating, chatting, washing, writing letters, etc. 'When they do a time log', says Sam Flowers, 'most people are amazed at how much time they waste.'

112

b Look at Kate's time log. Match the times to the pictures.

TIME LOG

TIME	ACTIVITY
7.00	Wake up; switch on radio; stay in bed.
7.15	Get up; shower/clean teeth.
7.45	Have breakfast.
8.00	Get dressed.
8.20	Leave for work.
9.00	Arrive at work; cup of coffee; John comes in; talk about TV programme that we both watched last night.
9.15	Go to have a word with Fred about tomorrow's meeting. He isn't there. Walk back to office.

9.30	Read morning's post.
10.00	Decide to start work.
10.15	Amanda phones. She's just got back from her holidays; chat.
10.30	Coffee break
10.50	Start work: computer isn't working. Phone engineer to explain fault.
11.20	Walk to the computer laboratory in the next building.
11.35	All the computers in the lab are being used.
11.45	Return to office. Computer engineer has arrived. He explains the problem.
12.00	Start typing letter.
12.30	Lunch time

4 Analyse Kate's time log.

a How much time did Kate spend doing each thing?

EXAMPLES

listening to the radio — *fifteen minutes*
having a shower, etc. — *thirty minutes*

b How much time did she actually spend working?

5 A consultant from TMS is commenting on Kate's time log.

a Complete his analysis of Kate's morning, using Kate's time log and these tenses: the past simple, the past continuous, the present perfect, the past perfect.

> 'OK, let's take a look at Kate's time log. What did she do in her morning? She _____ at work at 9.00. While she _____ a cup of coffee, John _____ . They _____ about a TV programme that they _____ the night before. At 9.15 Kate _____ to have a word with Fred about the meeting the next day, but Fred _____ there, so she _____ back to her office.
> After she _____ the morning's post, she _____ to start work. But Amanda _____ . She was back from her holiday. They _____ till 10.30. After the coffee break, Kate _____ work, but the computer _____ , so she _____ the engineer. Then she _____ to the computer laboratory, but all the computers _____ , so she _____ to the office. The computer engineer _____ . He _____ the problem.
> Kate _____ typing a letter at 12.00. At 12.30 she _____ to lunch.
> So what has Kate achieved in her morning's work? In four hours she has really only done two things: she _____ the morning's post and she _____ a letter. Not a lot for four hours!'

b ▣ *14.1* Listen and check.

6 You have decided to manage your time better.

a What are you going to do? Write down five ideas. How will each one save you time?

b Ask other people in the class what they are going to do.

c Compare your ideas.

7 If you could save one extra hour each day by managing your time better, what would you do with the extra hour?

a ▣ *14.2* Listen to four people talking about what they would do.

b Tick (✓) the things they mention.

☐ go to work later
☐ spend more time with the family
☐ start playing golf
☐ read more

☐ stay in bed longer
☐ learn a new language
☐ take more exercise
☐ relax

c ▣ *14.2* Listen again. What reasons do the people give?

d What would you do with an extra hour a day? Compare your ideas with a partner.

Vocabulary
Adjectives and nouns

We can form abstract nouns from many adjectives. This table shows some of the common noun endings.

adjective	noun	ending
sad	sadness	+ness
silent	silence	nt > nce
brave	bravery	+y
strong	strength	+th
dangerous	danger	no ending

1 Look at this list of adjectives.

> happy   important   honest   warm
> careful   long   lucky   different
> difficult   safe   selfish   respected
> thrilling   private   successful   mad

a Use a dictionary. Complete the chart with the adjectives and their nouns.

b Which nouns have a spelling change, or add an extra letter?

2 Choose nouns from the chart to complete these sentences. Discuss your choices with a partner.

1 _____ is more important than _____ .

2 _____ is important for _____ in a relationship.

3 _____ is important for _____ in a job.

4 A thing that I dislike in people is _____ .

5 Important qualities in a person are _____ and _____ .

Reading
Heroic, brave or just crazy?

1 **Look at the title and photographs. Discuss these questions.**
1 Why do war correspondents do their job?
2 Is it a necessary job? Why are people interested in war news?
3 What does the title say about them and their job?
4 Would you like to do it? Why/Why not?

2 **Read the article.**

a Which correspondents are mentioned?

b These statements are similar to what the correspondents say in the article. Write the correspondent's initials next to each statement.
1 ____ War reporters are a very exclusive group of people.
2 ____ Sometimes when it's really dangerous I wonder why I do it.
3 ____ You can't really show what's happening if you don't take some risks.
4 ____ Every reporter wants to be a foreign correspondent.
5 ____ All war reporters are a bit crazy.
6 ____ I often promise that I'll stop, but I know that I won't.
7 ____ I always carry a good luck message from my wife.
8 ____ The danger of war is exciting.
9 ____ I feel very proud that I can see important world events as they happen.

c Explain how you matched the statements and correspondents.

d Find all the words in the text associated with *war* and *the media*.

3 **Answer these questions.**
1 Which war is used to illustrate the dangers of the job?
2 Which other wars are mentioned?
3 Which of the correspondents do you think is the oldest? Why?
4 What happened to Martin Bell?
5 Which two news organizations are mentioned?
6 What do none of the correspondents believe?

4 **Do excitement and danger always go together? Can you think of other jobs that are exciting but not dangerous, or dangerous but not exciting?**

5 **Work in groups. Write an article about another job and why people do it. The article can be serious or humorous, about a real or an imaginary job.**

a First make notes on
• a typical activity in the job.
• the problems or difficulties of the job.
• why people do it.
• what qualities people need to do it.

b Write your article, using this format:

Paragraph 1 *You're … You're going to …* (Set the scene of someone about to do the job.)

Paragraph 2 *That's all in a day's work for a …* (Say what the job is and give the problems and difficulties of it.)

Paragraph 3 *So why do people do it?* (Give quotes from people about why they do the job.)

Paragraph 4 *Could you be a … ?* (Give the qualities you need for the job.)

Heroic, brave or just crazy?

You're near the front line of a battle. Around you shells are exploding. People are shooting from a house behind you. What are you doing there? You aren't a soldier. You aren't even carrying a gun. You're standing in front of a camera and you're telling the TV viewers what is happening.

Sandy Gall, respected reporter

It's all in a day's work for a war correspondent, and it can be very dangerous. In the first two years of the conflict in former Yugoslavia, 28 reporters and photographers were killed. Hundreds more were injured, including the BBC's Martin Bell. What kind of people put themselves in danger to bring pictures to our TV screens and stories to our newspapers? Why do they do it?

'I don't know whether we're macho or masochists,' says ITN's Michael Nicholson. 'I think it's every young reporter's dream to be a foreign correspondent - that's where you find the excitement. So when the first opportunity comes, you take it even if it is a war.' Jeremy Bowen from the BBC agrees. 'I don't think we like the danger, but it gives you a certain thrill. After a while other stories become a bit dull.'

Although they work for different organizations, war reporters help each other. 'As a war reporter,' says Michael Nicholson, 'you become a member of a very exclusive club and you depend on each other.' One of the most respected members of that club is Sandy Gall. He's reported on several conflicts including the Suez Crisis of 1956, Vietnam, Afghanistan and the Gulf War. Sandy says, 'We're all a bit mad, if not when we start, then certainly by the end.'

Martin Bell with a film crew, during the Gulf War

They all think that their job is important. 'I don't like the danger at all,' says Penny Marshall, 'but it's the only way to get an honest report. We aren't brave, because you don't really think about the danger when you're in it, but you have to be calm.' For Kate Adie the danger isn't the important thing. She describes her job as a privilege. 'You're seeing history in the making,' she says.

Kate Adie, dressed for action

But there are moments of terror. Jeremy Bowen again: 'Yes, when you're lying on the ground and bullets are flying past your ears, you think: "What the hell am I doing here? I'm not going to do this again." But that feeling goes after a while and when the next war starts, you'll be there.'

'None of us believes that we're going to die,' adds Michael Nicholson. But he always carries a lucky charm with him. It was given to him by his wife for his first war. It's a card which says, 'Take care of yourself.' Does he ever think about dying? 'Oh, many times, and every time it happens you look to the sky and say to God, "If you get me out of this, I promise I'll never do it again". You can almost hear God laughing, because you know He doesn't believe you.'

Listening and speaking
Small talk

1 **Read about the woman in the photographs.**

> Annette Van der Alst lives in a small town near Brussels in Belgium. She is on a two-day business trip to Oxford. She has got a reservation at the Carling Hotel. This is her third visit to Oxford.

a Look at the conversation.

b Some of Annette's part of the conversation is missing. What do you think she says? Look at **Conversation pieces** for some ideas.

Taxi driver   Where to, miss?

Annette   The Carling Hotel, please.

Taxi driver   Certainly. Have you got any luggage?

Annette   Yes, I've got this suitcase.

Taxi driver   Right. I'll just see to that. Now where are you staying again, miss?

Annette   _____

Taxi driver   Right. A bit grey today, isn't it?

Annette   _____

Taxi driver   It's a bit grey today, the weather. It's not very nice. You know. Dull.

Annette   _____

Taxi driver   Still, at least it isn't raining.

Annette   _____

Taxi driver   Is this your first time here?

Annette   _____

Taxi driver   Are you here on business or on holiday?

Annette   _____

Taxi driver   How long are you staying?

Annette   _____

Taxi driver   Well, I hope you aren't in a hurry.

Annette   _____

Taxi driver   Well, the traffic's terrible. This is only my second run today.

Annette   _____

Taxi driver   There are just too many vehicles on the road.

Annette   _____

Taxi driver   Where are you from, then?

Annette   _____

Taxi driver   Oh, yes. Whereabouts?

Annette   _____

Taxi driver   Oh right. Well, here we are. That's £8.25, please, miss.

Annette   Here you are. Keep the change.

Taxi driver   Thanks a lot, miss.

2 📼 *14.3* **You will hear the complete conversation. Listen and check your ideas.**

Conversation pieces: Small talk

a Two common small talk themes in Britain are the weather and traffic! What do strangers talk to each other about in your country?

b Look at these common expressions.

Talking about the weather:

Fine	
Warm	
Nice	
Lovely	
A bit grey	*today, isn't it?*
A bit windy	
Cold	
Wet	
Terrible	

Talking about the traffic:

The traffic's	*all right*	
	bad	*today, isn't it?*
	terrible	

Agreeing:
Yes, that's true.
I suppose you're right.
Yes, I agree.
Yes, I suppose so.

Asking for clarification:
Why's that?
Pardon?
What do you mean?
I'm sorry. I didn't get that.

c Look at tapescript 14.3 and practise the conversation with a partner. Add your own ideas for extending the conversation.

3 **An English-speaking visitor has arrived in your country. Work with a partner. One of you is the visitor and one is a taxi driver. Make the conversation.**

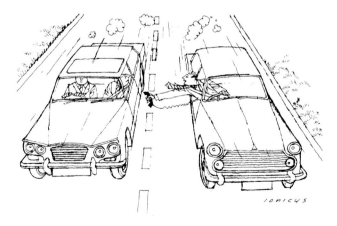

'It's for you.'

Pronunciation
Revision

1 **In some of these groups, one of the words does not have the same vowel sound as the other two words in the group.**

a Circle the words that have a different vowel sound.

1	thumb	come	home
2	brave	same	day
3	done	son	one
4	put	book	door
5	push	rush	pull
6	climb	sign	time
7	warm	saw	car
8	can't	want	what
9	walk	tall	shall
10	so	do	to
11	cheap	feel	hit
12	bought	pound	out

b 📼 *14.4* Listen and check.

2 **Look at these sentences.**

a Mark the stressed syllables and draw the intonation curves.

1 What shall we do this evening?

2 Why is your jacket on the floor?

3 I'm going to see my friend.

4 Do you want a cup of coffee?

5 Is it windy today?

6 I suppose you're right.

7 Is that a good idea?

8 Where would you like to live?

b 📼 *14.5* Listen and check.

3 **What does this say?**
/jʊv riːtʃt ðə jend əv ðə bʊk/
/həv jʊ lɜːnt ə lɒt/
/gʊd lʌk wɪð jə nekst jɪər əv ɪŋglɪʃ/

Extension:
Reading and listening
Summertime Blues

1 Look at the song.

a Answer the questions.

1 How old do you think the singer is?

2 Why has he got the blues?

3 Tick (✓) which people he mentions.

☐ his boss

☐ his girlfriend's mother

☐ the neighbours

☐ his sister

☐ his parents

☐ his girlfriend

☐ his congressman

☐ the president

b What do you think the missing words are?

c 📼 *14.6* Listen and check your ideas.

2 Find American English expressions in the song that mean the same as these:

I'm going to …
there isn't a …
to shout
no chance
you have to …
Mum and Dad
did no work at all
holiday
Member of Parliament

3 Answer these questions.

1 What is the singer going to make a fuss about?

2 How does his boss make his life difficult?

3 What does he want to do?

4 What does he have to do?

5 Why can't he use the car?

6 What is he going to do for two weeks?

7 Why won't his congressman help him?

4 What things give you the blues? What would you complain about in a song?

I'm a-gonna raise a fuss, I'm
_____ raise a holler,
About working all summer just to try
to make a _____ .
Every time I _____ my baby
and try to make a date,
My boss says, 'No dice, son. You gotta
_____ late.'
Sometimes I _____ what I'm
a-gonna do,
But there ain't no cure for the
_____ Blues.

Well, my mom and poppa told me, 'Son
you gotta make some _____ ,
If you want to use the _____
to go driving next Sunday.'
Well I _____ go to work, I
told the boss I was sick.
'Now you _____ use the car,
'cos you didn't work a lick.'
Sometimes I wonder _____ I'm
a-gonna do,
But there _____ no cure for
the Summertime Blues.

I'm gonna take two weeks, I'm gonna
_____ a fine vacation.
I'm gonna take my problem to the
United _____ .
Well I _____ my congressman
and he said, 'No.
I'd like to _____ you, son,
but you're too young to vote.'
_____ I wonder what I'm a-
gonna do,
But there ain't no _____ for
the Summertime Blues.

Summertime Blues

Reflecting on Learning 1:
Your aims

What do you want to achieve in this course?

a Think about these things.
- Why are you studying English?
- What things do you need or want to do in English?

b Look at this list.
- Listening
- Speaking
- Reading
- Writing
- Pronunciation
- Grammar
- Vocabulary

What do you think you can do well in English?
What do you find difficult?
Discuss with your partner, and then with the class.

Reflecting on Learning 2:
Recording vocabulary

A useful way to record vocabulary is to make your own dictionary.

a Look at the example from a German student's notebook. What kind of information does he include?

Unit 1   20th September

cupboard (n) /ˈkʌbəd/: Schrank

armchair (n) /ˈɑːmtʃeə/: Sessel – sit in an
                                                armchair

to chat (v) /tʃæt/: plaudern
a chat (n) – to have a chat

b You can organize your vocabulary records in different ways. Which of these do you think are useful? Why?
- by parts of speech (nouns, verbs, etc.)
- alphabetically
- in word families
- in the order that they are in the book
- by situation (e.g. at the shops)
- by topic (e.g. clothes, money)

Reflecting on Learning 3:
Parts of speech

It can be useful to know the parts of speech. They can help you to use a dictionary and a grammar book more easily.

a These are the main parts of speech.

conjunction   verb   adjective   pronoun

When John sits in his new car, he smiles happily.

preposition   noun   adverb

b Find examples of each of these parts of speech in this sentence.
Sally's young son cut his hand badly, so she took him to the hospital.

Reflecting on Learning 4:
Using dictionaries

A good dictionary is a great help in studying a language, especially outside the class. It can help you with meaning, spelling, grammar and pronunciation. At pre-intermediate level you can use a bilingual dictionary or an English–English dictionary, like the *Oxford Elementary Learner's Dictionary*.

Look at this extract from the *Oxford Pocket Spanish Dictionary*.

pronunciation   part of speech   translation
                (*n*=noun, *vt/vi*=verb,
                a=adjective, etc.)

house /haʊs/ ◆ *n* (*pl* **-s** /ˈhaʊzɪz/) **1** casa **2** (*Teat*) sala de espectáculos: *There was a full house.* Se llenó al completo. **LOC on the house** cortesía de la casa *Ver tb* MOVE ◆ /haʊz/ *vt* alojar, albergar

expressions and phrases   example sentences

It is a good idea to use a dictionary which has this information, and which uses the IPA to show pronunciation.

Reflecting on Learning 5:
Making mistakes

Mistakes are a natural part of learning a language. We make mistakes for several reasons. Here are some possibilities.
- It's different from your language.
- It's similar to your language but not exactly the same.
- You don't understand the rule.
- It's an exception to the rule.
- You don't know, so you guess.

Look at your work in this unit. Find five mistakes that you made. Why did you make them? Discuss your ideas with other members of the class.

Reflecting on Learning 6:
Nouns

a This is the normal pattern of a sentence in English:

subject	verb	object
Jane	likes	films.
My sister Jane	loves	old, black and white films.

The subject and object are normally nouns or noun phrases.

b Nouns often have an article. There are two kinds of article.
Definite article   *the*
Indefinite article   *a/an, some/any*

c Nouns have two forms – singular and plural. To make plurals we usually add -*s*.
EXAMPLE
dog   *dogs*

But there are some exceptions. What are the plurals of these words, and how are they pronounced?
fly, watch, knife, tomato, foot, key, man, glass, woman, child, mouse, brush
➤ Check in **Grammar Reference 2.2**.

d Nouns can be replaced by pronouns. Change the repeated noun in the second sentence into a pronoun.
Where's the cat? I can't find the cat.
Unlike nouns, some pronouns change their form depending on whether they are a subject or an object. Complete this list.

Subject pronouns	Object pronouns
I	_____
You	_____
He	_____
She	_____
It	_____
We	_____
They	_____

Reflecting on Learning 7:
Verbs

A sentence must have a verb. All verbs must have a subject, except for imperatives.

a These sentences illustrate different types of verb in English. Match the sentences to the correct grammatical term.

I **sleep** for eight hours a night.	a modal verb
Go to bed!	an auxiliary verb
Do you like paella?	a phrasal verb
I **saw** her yesterday.	a transitive verb
We **should** go.	an intransitive verb
John **picked up** the book.	an imperative

b Give one more example of each item.
c How are the grammatical terms written in the dictionary?

Reflecting on Learning 8:
Correction

Discuss these questions.
1 Do you like it when your teacher corrects your mistakes
  ● when you are talking?
  ● in your written work?
2 Does correction help you? Why/Why not?
3 What do you do with the corrections?
4 What kind of correction do you find helpful/unhelpful?

Reflecting on Learning 9:
Dealing with unknown words

a As you read, you will often meet an unknown word. What should you do?

1 Try not to use a dictionary immediately.
2 Try to get the general meaning of the text first.
3 Try one of these strategies.
  ● Ignore the word. Some words aren't important to the meaning.
  ● Try to work out the meaning of the word from the context.
  ● Guess the meaning and continue reading.

b At the end of the reading, look back at the unknown words and check them in a dictionary. Did the strategies work?

Reflecting on Learning 10:
Pair and group work

In this course you often work in pairs or groups. What do you think about working in this way?
Make a list of the advantages and disadvantages of pair and group work.
Discuss your ideas with other members of the class.

Reflecting on Learning 11:
Ways of learning

You have worked in many different ways so far in the course. Which ways do you prefer?
a Look at this list.
  ● grammar exercises   ● reading comprehension
  ● roleplays   ● pronunciation practice
  ● discussions   ● writing exercises
  ● dictionary work   ● group work
  ● learning words   ● listening
  ● pairwork   ● games

b Complete the table, putting items in each column.

I like	
I don't like	
most useful	
least useful	

c Discuss your ideas with the class. What do your choices tell you about your learning style?

Reflecting on Learning 12:
The verb *to have*

The verb *to have* has different uses.
a Match the uses to the correct examples.

Uses	Examples
a main verb	*She's got fair hair.*
an auxiliary verb	*We have lunch at 1.00.*
with *got* to show possession	*I've been to London.*

b For each, how we do form
  ● positive statements?   ● questions?
  ● negative statements?   ● short answers?

0.1 *There is/there are*

Positive

There	's (is)	a pen a glass	on the table.
	are	five pens two glasses	

We use *there is* with singular nouns and *there are* with plural nouns.
Note: There is no short form for *there are*.

Negative

There	isn't (is not)	a pen a glass	on the table.
	aren't (are not)	any pens any glasses	

Questions

Is	there	a pen a glass	on the table?
Are		any pens any glasses	

Short answers

Yes, there | is.
are.

No, there | isn't.
(is not.)
aren't.
(are not.)

1.1 The present simple tense

Form

Positive

I We You They	live work	in London.
He She It	lives works	here.

- **Spelling**
  General rule: In the third person singular we add *-s* to the infinitive.
  Exceptions: When the verb ends in *-ss, -sh, -ch, -z* or *-o*, we add *-es*.
  miss/misses *wash/washes* *catch/catches*
  buzz/buzzes *go/goes*
  When the verb ends in consonant + *y*, we change the *-y* to *-ies*.
  hurry/hurries *marry/marries*
- **Pronunciation**
  General rule: We pronounce the final *-s* as /z/.
  comes /kʌmz/ *goes* /gəʊz/
  Exceptions: After /t/, /p/, /f/, and /k/, we pronounce the final *-s* as /s/.
  cuts /kʌts/ *stops* /stɒps/ *coughs* /kɒfs/ *looks* /lʊks/

  When the verb ends in *-ges, -ches, -sses, -ses, -zes* or *-shes*, we pronounce the final syllable /ɪz/.
  changes /tʃeɪndʒɪz/ *pushes* /pʊʃɪz/

Negative

I We You They	don't (do not)	live in London.
He She It	doesn't (does not)	work here.

Questions

Do	I we you they	live in London?
Does	he she it	work here?

Short answers

Yes, | I
we
you
they | do.
he
she
it | does.

No, | I
we
you
they | don't.
(do not.)
he
she
it | doesn't.
(does not.)

Note: In negatives and questions we use the infinitive form of the verb.

She doesn't **like** wine.   NOT *She doesn't likes wine.*
Does he **play** football?   NOT *Does he plays football?*

Use

We use the present simple tense to

- describe regular events.
  I get up at seven o'clock (every day).
  We usually meet after work.

- describe general truths and states.
  The Earth goes round the Sun.
  Exercise helps your heart.
  She plays the piano.
  They live in Manchester.

1.2 *should/shouldn't*

Form

Positive + negative

I He She	should	clean the windows.
We You They	shouldn't (should not)	watch so much television.

Questions

Should	I he she we you they	make the bed? tell him?

Short answers

Yes, | I
he
she
we
you
they | should.

No, | | shouldn't.
(should not.)

Use

We use *should/shouldn't* to

- say what we think is the right thing for people to do.
  *You **shouldn't** drive so fast, it's dangerous.*

- give advice.
  *If you're ill, you **should** go to the doctor.*
  *What do you think I **should** do?*

2.1 The present continuous tense

Form

We make the present continuous tense with the verb *to be* and the *-ing* form of the verb.

Positive

I	'm (am)	reading a book.
He She It	's (is)	raining.
We You They	're (are)	going to the shops.

Negative

I	'm not (am not)	reading a book.
He She It	isn't (is not)	raining.
We You They	aren't (are not)	going to the shops.

Note: The short forms *He's/She's/It's/We're/They're not* are also possible.

Questions

Am	I	reading a book?
Is	he she it	raining?
Are	we you they	going to the shops?

Short answers

Yes,	I	am.
	he she it	is.
	we you they	are.

No,	I	'm not. (am not.)
	he she it	isn't. (is not.)
	we you they	aren't. (are not.)

Note: The short forms *No, he's/she's/it's not* and *No, we're/you're/they're not* are also possible.

● **Spelling**

For the spelling rules for present participles see Gerunds (section 10.2).

Use

We use the present continuous tense to

● say what is happening at the moment.
We're watching TV at the moment.
'Where's Jane?' 'She's having a bath.'

● describe a temporary state.
I'm staying with friends for the weekend.
I'm living with my parents until I find a house.

● describe a future arrangement.
I'm going to London tomorrow.
She's meeting her boyfriend this afternoon.

Present simple and present continuous

Look at these sentences. In each pair one is right and one is wrong.

1 I'm going to the cinema tomorrow evening. ✓
I'm going to the cinema every day. ✗
2 She gets up at 6.00 every day. ✓
She's getting up at 6.00 every day. ✗
3 **A** Where's John? **B** He's playing tennis. ✓
A Where's John? **B** He plays tennis. ✗
4 I'm staying with my parents this week. ✓
I stay with my parents this week. ✗
5 Vegetarians don't eat meat. ✓
Vegetarians aren't eating meat. ✗
6 **A** What do you do? **B** I'm a teacher. ✓
A What do you do? **B** I watch a film. ✗

Look at the **Use** sections for the present simple (section 1.1) and the present continuous and check the rules.

2.2 Plurals

a To make most plurals we add *-s* to the noun.
a dog *two dogs*
a girl *three girls*
a day *four days*

b With words that end in *-ch, -ss, -sh* or *-o*, we add *-es*.
a watch *two watches*   a brush *four brushes*
a dress *three dresses*   a tomato *five tomatoes*

When the plural ends in *-ches, -sses, -ses, -shes* or *-ges*, we pronounce the *-es* ending /ɪz/.
watches /wɒtʃɪz/   crashes /kræʃɪz/
glasses /glɑːsɪz/   badges /bædʒɪz/
noses /nəʊzɪz/

c With words that end in a consonant + *y*, we change the *-y* to *-ies*
a fly *two flies*
a baby *three babies*

But with words that end in a vowel + *y* we add *-s*.
a day *two days*   a key *three keys*

d With some words that end in *-f* or *-fe*, the plural ending is *-ves*.
a knife *two knives*   a loaf *three loaves*

e Some words that contain *-oo-* change to *-ee-*.
a foot *two feet*   a tooth *three teeth*

f Some plurals are irregular.
a man *two men*   a woman *three women*
a child *four children*   a mouse *five mice*

We use *this/that* with singular nouns and *these/those* with plural nouns.
this book   *these* books   *that* child   *those* children

2.3 *have/have got*

Form: *have*

Positive

I We You They	have	two cars.
He She It	has	a good memory.

Negative

| I
We
You
They | don't have
(do not have) | two cars. |
| He
She
It | doesn't have
(does not have) | a good memory. |

Questions

| Do | I
we
you
they | have | two cars? |
| Does | he
she
it | | a good memory? |

Short answers

| Yes, | I
we
you
they | do. | No, | I
we
you
they | don't.
(do not.) |
| | he
she
it | does. | | he
she
it | doesn't.
(does not.) |

Form: *have got*

Positive

| I
We
You
They | 've
(have) | got | two cars. |
| He
She
It | 's
(has) | | a good memory. |

Negative

| I
We
You
They | haven't
(have not) | got | two cars. |
| He
She
It | hasn't
(has not) | | a good memory. |

Questions

| Have | I
we
you
they | got | two cars? |
| Has | he
she
it | | a good memory? |

Short answers

| Yes, | I
we
you
they | have. | No, | I
we
you
they | haven't.
(have not.) |
| | he
she
it | has. | | he
she
it | hasn't.
(has not.) |

Use

- We can use *have got* or *have* to talk about possession. In British English we often use *have got* in conversation. It is informal. *Have got* is only used in the present tense.
  We've got a dog.

- *Have* can be more formal, and we often use it in writing. It is the form most often used in American English. *Have* is used in all tenses.
  My father had three brothers. (past)
  When I'm rich I'll have two houses. (will future)

- To talk about activities we can only use *have*.
  I have lunch at 12.30.   NOT *I've got lunch at 12.30.*
  John's having a shower.   NOT *John's having got a shower.*

3.1 The past simple tense

Form
The verb *to be*
Positive

| I
He
She
It | was | in the office last week. |
| We
You
They | were | ill yesterday. |

Negative

| I
He
She
It | wasn't
(was not) | in the office last week. |
| We
You
They | weren't
(were not) | ill yesterday. |

Questions

| Was | I
he
she
it | in the office last week? |
| Were | we
you
they | ill yesterday? |

Short answers

| Yes, | I
he
she
it | was. | No, | I
he
she
it | wasn't.
(was not.) |
| | we
you
they | were. | | we
you
they | weren't.
(were not.) |

Regular and irregular verbs
Positive

General rule: To make the past simple tense of regular verbs we add *-ed* to the infinitive. It is the same for all persons.

I watched television last night.
It happened yesterday.
You looked out of the window.

- **Spelling**
  When the verb ends in *-e*, we add *-d*.
  like   *liked*   use   *used*

When the verb ends in a short vowel and a single consonant, we double the consonant and add -ed.

stop *stopped*   drag *dragged*

When the verb ends in consonant +*y* we change the -*y* to -*ied*.

try *tried*   marry *married*

- **Pronunciation**
  General rule: We pronounce the final -*d* as /d/.
  pulled /pʊld/, *approved* /əpruːvd/

  Exceptions: After /p/, /k/, /tʃ/, /ʃ/ and /s/ we pronounce the final -*d* as /t/.
  cooked /kʊkt/ *stopped* /stɒpt/ *reached* /riːtʃt/ *missed* /mɪst/
  When the verb ends in -*t* or -*d* we pronounce the final syllable /ɪd/.
  wanted /wɒntɪd/ *needed* /niːdɪd/

Many common verbs have an irregular past form. (See the list of irregular verbs on the inside back cover.) It is the same form for all persons.

verb	past simple
do	I **did** it yesterday.
see	We **saw** him last week.
come	She **came** to the party.

Negative

I He She It We You They	didn't (did not)	like the film. go to the party. steal the money.

Questions

Did	I he she it we you they	like the film? go to the party? steal the money?

Short answers

Yes,	I he she it we you they	did.
No,		didn't. (did not.)

Note: In negatives and questions we use the infinitive of the verb.
She **didn't like** the film. NOT ~~She didn't liked the film.~~
Did you **go** to London? NOT ~~Did you went to London?~~

Note: Negatives, questions, and short answers are the same for all persons and both regular and irregular verbs.

Use

We use the past simple tense to describe
- a completed action in the past.

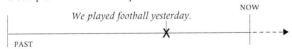
We played football yesterday.

- a completed situation in the past.

I lived in Paris from 1988 to 1993.

- a repeated action in the past.

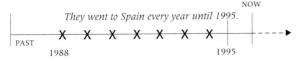
They went to Spain every year until 1995.

See the past continuous tense (section 6.1) and the present perfect tense (section 7.1).

3.2 Adverbs and adjectives

Form
Adverbs

Most adverbs end in -*ly*.

adjective	adverb
brave	bravely
loud	loudly
quick	quickly
dangerous	dangerously
bad	badly

Some adverbs are irregular.

adjective	adverb
good	well
fast	fast
hard	hard

Adjectives

We put adjectives in front of the noun.

	adjective	noun
a	new	car
two	green	apples
	blue	eyes

Adjectives do not change.

a	**big**	house
two	**big**	houses

We use *an* in front of an adjective that begins with a vowel.
an old man
an easy exam

Use

- Adverbs describe verbs.
  *You can do this exercise **easily**.* (*Easily* describes *do*.)

- Adjectives describe nouns.
  *This is an **easy** exercise.* (*Easy* describes *exercise*.)

4.1 The future with *will*

Form
Positive + negative

I He She It	'll (will)	get in touch.
We You They	won't (will not)	be there.

Questions

Will	I he she it we you they	get in touch? be there?

Short answers

Yes,	I he she it we you they	will.
No,		won't. (will not.)

Use

We use the future with *will*
- to make predictions or general statements about the future.
  In the next century the world will run out of oil.
  This medicine won't do you any good.

- to express a decision made at the moment of speaking.
  A *The television's very loud.*   **A** *Is Peter going to the party?*
  B *OK. I'll turn it down.*   **B** *I don't know. I'll give him a ring.*

- in the main clause of a first conditional.
  If you drink this, you'll feel better. (See section 4.2)

Will and the present continuous for the future

Look at these sentences. In each pair one is right and one is wrong.

1 **A** What are you doing this evening?
  B I'm going to a party. ✓
  A What will you do this evening?
  B I'll go to a party. ✗
2 **A** It's cold in here.
  B I'll close the window. ✓
  A It's cold in here.
  B I'm closing the window. ✗
3 Soon everybody will have a computer. ✓
  Soon everybody is having a computer. ✗
4 You'll feel better if you take an aspirin. ✓
  You're feeling better if you take an aspirin. ✗
5 **A** Have you got any plans for the weekend?
  B Yes, I'm visiting my brother in Scotland. ✓
  B Yes, I'll visit my brother in Scotland. ✗

Look at the **Use** sections for *will* and the present continuous (section 2.1) and check the rules.

4.2 First conditionals (*if* clauses)

Form

We use the present simple tense in the *if* clause and the future with *will* in the main clause.
*If I **see** him, I'**ll tell** him.*
*She'**ll be** hungry if she **doesn't eat** something.*

We use the same construction with time clauses.
*We'**ll wait** here until he **arrives**.*
*You'**ll have** more information when Sarah **gets** here.*
*I'**ll leave** before it **starts** to rain.*

Use

First conditionals predict the effects of a real or probable action or event.
If you lie in the sun too long, you'll get sunburnt.
We won't go out if it rains.

5.1 Comparatives and superlatives

	adjective	comparative	superlative
one syllable	tall cold	taller colder	the tallest the coldest
one syllable; short vowel + one consonant	hot thin big	hotter thinner bigger	the hottest the thinnest the biggest
two syllables; consonant + *y*	heavy pretty	heavier prettier	the heaviest the prettiest
two or more syllables	modern interesting	more modern more interesting	the most modern the most interesting
irregular	good bad far	better worse further	the best the worst the furthest

A comparative adjective is often followed by *than*.
*Russia is bigger **than** Canada.*

as ... as ... can be used to make comparisons.
*Her house is **as big as** mine.*
*Silver isn't **as expensive as** gold.*

In the negative *so ... as ...* is also possible.
*Silver isn't **so expensive as** gold.*

5.2 Clothes

The names of some clothes are always plural.
jeans   trousers   shorts

These words take plural articles and plural verbs.
These trousers are too short.
I need some new jeans.

a pair of

When we talk about a quantity of clothes, we must use *pair(s) of* with words that are already plural.
*three T-shirts, two **pairs of** jeans, a **pair of** shoes, two skirts, four **pairs of** knickers*

6.1 The past continuous tense

Form
Positive

I He She It	was	having a shower.
We You They	were	waiting for a bus.

Negative

I He She It	wasn't (was not)	having a shower.
We You They	weren't (were not)	waiting for a bus.

Questions

Was	I he she it	having a shower?
Were	we you they	waiting for a bus?

Short answers

	I he she it	was.			I he she it	wasn't. (was not.)
Yes,	we you they	were.	No,		we you they	weren't. (were not.)

Use

The past continuous tense describes a continuous or unfinished activity in the past.
I was watching TV at 8.00 last night.

Past simple and past continuous

We often use the past continuous tense with the past simple tense. The clauses are usually joined by *while, as* or *when.*

While he was having a bath, the telephone rang.

As I was going to the shops, I saw my friend.

We were driving to the airport when the accident happened.

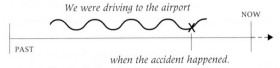

when the accident happened.

Compare these two sentences.
While he was having a bath, the telephone rang.

When he heard the phone, he got out of the bath.

The first sentence has a past continuous tense to set the scene and a past simple tense to say what happened. The second sentence has two past simple tenses. One action happened after the other.

7.1 The present perfect tense

Form

Positive

I We You They	've (have)	bought a new car.
He She It	's (has)	gone.

Note: After words ending in /s/, /z/, /tʃ/, /ʃ/, /dʒ/ we do not normally use the short form of *has.* We use the full form. In speech this is pronounced /(h)əz)/.

Negative

I We You They	haven't (have not)	bought a new car.
He She It	hasn't (has not)	gone.

Questions

Have	I we you they	bought a new car?
Has	he she it	gone?

Short answers

Yes,	I we you they	have.	No,	I we you they	haven't. (have not.)
	he she it	has.		he she it	hasn't. (has not.)

We make the present perfect tense with the verb *have/has* and the past participle of the verb. We form regular participles in the same way as the regular past simple tense (see section 3.1).
wait   *waited*   stay   *stayed*

A lot of common verbs have an irregular past participle.
go   *gone*   write   *written*

(See the list of irregular verbs on the inside back cover.)

Use

The present perfect links the past with the present.

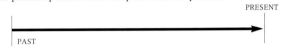

We use it
● when we are referring to a time frame that comes up to the present.
I've been to Egypt three times. (Up till now I've been there three times.)
Have you had a busy day today? (We are still in the time frame of 'today'.)

● when we are interested in the present result of a past action.
Elizabeth's bought a new car. (She has a new car now.)
We've had our lunch. (We're not hungry now.)

● when a situation or activity started in the past and continues in the present.
We've lived here for two years. (And we still live here now.)

been/gone

Be and *go* have a particular meaning in the present perfect tense.
*She's **gone** to London.* (She is still in London. She hasn't come back yet.)
*She's **been** to London.* (She has come back.)

We use *be* when we are talking about our experiences.
*Have you ever **been** to India?*
*We've **been** to Scotland three times.*

Present perfect and past simple

Compare the present perfect with the past simple tense. We use the past simple

● when we are interested in the action or the time of the action, not the effect.
She's bought a new car. She bought it last week.
We've had our lunch. We went to that new café in town.

● when the action finished in the past.
We've lived here since 1988. Before that I lived in London.

● when we are referring to a time frame that ended in the past.
I've been to Egypt three times. Last year I was in Cairo.
Have you had a busy day today? Yes, but yesterday was worse.

Note: When there is a past time reference (*in 1987, two days ago, yesterday*), you must use the past simple tense, not the present perfect.

7.2 *for/since*

We often use *for* and *since* with the present perfect tense. We use *for* with a period of time. We use *since* with a point in time.

| *I've lived here* | *for two years.* |
| | *since 1991.* |

> **Present perfect, present simple and present continuous**
>
> Look at these sentences. Some are right and some are wrong.
> 1 How long have you lived in France? ✓
>   How long do you live in France? ✗
>   How long are you living in France? ✗
> 2 I've been a teacher since 1988. ✓
>   I'm a teacher since 1988. ✗
> 3 He's worked in a bank for ten years. ✓
>   He works in a bank for ten years. ✗
> 4 How long have you had your car? ✓
>   How long do you have your car? ✗
>   How long are you having your car? ✗
>
> Look at the **Use** sections for the present perfect, the present simple (section 1.1) and the present continuous (section 2.1) and check the rules.

8.1 Expressing quantity

some/any

Some and *any* are the indefinite articles for plural nouns and uncountable nouns (see below).
We use *some* with positive statements.
*I need **some** new jeans.*

We use *any* with negative statements and questions.
*We haven't got **any** books.*
*Have you got **any** money?*

Countable and uncountable nouns

Some nouns are countable. They have a singular and a plural form.
*I've got a new **record**.*
*Here are some **records** for you.*

*I need a **stamp** for this letter.*
*Have you got any **stamps**?*

Some nouns are uncountable. They have no plural form. They can't take the singular article *a/an*. They use *some* or *any*.
*I need **some bread**.*
*I've got **some information** for you.*
*Have you got **any money**?*

These things are usually uncountable:
drinks: *tea, beer, wine, water, coffee, milk*
food which you only eat part of: *fish, bread, cheese, ham, meat*
things which you only use part of: *toothpaste, soap, shampoo*
materials: *paper, wood, wool, plastic*
some general words: *information, music, money*

Use *How many?* with countable nouns and *How much?* with uncountable nouns.

***How many** sandwiches do we need?*
***How much** cheese have we got left?*

8.2 *used to*

Form

Positive + negative

| I He She | used to | live in London. |
| It We You They | didn't use to (did not use to) | smoke. / have long hair. |

Questions

| Did | I he she it we you they | use to | live in London? smoke? have long hair? |

Short answers

| Yes, | I he she it we you they | did. |
| No, | | didn't. (did not.) |

Use

We use *used to*
- to express a habit in the past (which is no longer true in the present).
  *I **used to** play tennis every day, but I don't now.*

- to express a state in the past.

  | *She **used to** live in Sydney* | *but she now lives in Melbourne.* | NOW |
  | PAST | | |

Note: The past simple can also be used to express habits and states in the past. Only the past simple can be used for individual actions in the past.
Last night we went to the cinema.

Note: *used to* can only be used to talk about the past. To talk about habits and states in the present we use the present simple tense.
I play tennis every day.
She lives in Melbourne.

9.1 *would*

Form

Positive + negative

| I He She It | 'd (would) | like to live alone. |
| We You They | wouldn't (would not) | steal from a friend. |

Questions

| Would | I he she it we you they | like to live alone? steal from a friend? |

Short answers

| Yes, | I he she it we you they | would. |
| No, | | wouldn't. (would not.) |

Use

We use *would* to

- talk about improbable or impossible situations.
  I'd like to live alone. (But I live with six other people.)
  She'd be a good politician. (But she works in a bank.)

- make polite offers.
  ***Would** you like a cup of coffee?*
  ***Would** you like to go to the cinema?*

9.2 Second conditionals (*if* clauses)

Form

In second conditionals we use the conditional form in the main clause and the past tense in the *if* clause.
If I saw a ghost, I'd faint.
I'd buy a beautiful house if I had enough money.

Use

Second conditionals describe unreal, improbable or imaginary situations.
What would you do if you saw an accident?
If we won a lot of money, we'd spend it all.
If I had my life again, I wouldn't make the same mistakes.

Note: First and second conditionals both refer to the present or the future. The difference is how probable the action or situation is.
If I win the competition, I'll buy a new car.
(I think it is possible that I will win.)
If I won the competition, I'd buy a new car.
(I think it is improbable.)

We never use *will* or *would* in the *if* clause.
If I see him I'll tell him.   NOT *If I will see him...*
If I had the time I'd help you.   NOT *If I would have the time...*

10.1 The future with *going to*

Form

Positive

I	'm (am)		watch TV.
He She It	's (is)	going to	work.
We You They	're (are)		play tennis.

Negative

I	'm not (am not)		watch TV.
He She It	isn't (is not)	going to	work.
We You They	aren't (are not)		play tennis.

Questions

Am	I		watch TV?
Is	he she it	going to	work?
Are	we you they		play tennis?

Short answers

Yes,	I	am.
	he she it	is.
	we you they	are.

No,	I	'm not. (am not.)
	he she it	isn't. (is not.)
	we you they	aren't. (are not.)

Use

We use *going to* to

- talk about plans and intentions.
  *I'm **going to** buy a new car next week.*
  *I'm **going to** paint the living-room this weekend.*

- talk about things that we can see or feel about the future.
  *I feel terrible – I think I'm **going to** be sick.*
  *Look at those clouds! It's **going to** rain.*

going to and *will* for the future

Look at these sentences. In each pair one is right and one is wrong.

1   Oh no! He's lost control! He's going to crash! ✓
    Oh no! He's lost control! He'll crash! ✗
2   **A** I've got a terrible headache.
    B Oh dear. I'll get you some aspirin. ✓
    B Oh dear. I'm going to get you some aspirin. ✗
3   **A** Why have you got all that money?
    B I'm going to buy my Christmas presents. ✓
    B I'll buy my Christmas presents. ✗

Look at the **Use** sections for *going to* and *will* (section 4.1) and check the rules.

10.2 Gerunds

Form

- Spelling

  Basic rule: We add *-ing* to the infinitive.

wash	*washing*
read	*reading*
hurry	*hurrying*

  Exceptions: for verbs that end in *-e*, we remove the *-e* and add *-ing*.

drive	*driving*	use	*using*

  For verbs with a short vowel and only one consonant, we double the consonant and add *-ing*.

swim	*swimming*	sit	*sitting*

Use

A gerund is the *-ing* form of a verb.

We use gerunds as subjects or objects.
***Skiing** can be dangerous.*
*I like **travelling** by plane.*

Certain verbal expressions take a gerund.
*Would you mind **going** to the bank for me?*
*I don't mind **doing** that.*
*Do you fancy **watching** a video?*

Compare this to other expressions which take the infinitive.
*Do you think you could **go** to the bank for me?*
*I don't want **to do** that.*
*Would you like **to watch** a video?*

You'll have some time to relax if you're tired after the journey.

If you enjoy the show, we'll give you two free tickets for your friends.

If you want to meet the stars of the show, we'll take you backstage.

Our limousine will take you for a city tour if you want to see London by night.

We'll take you back to the hotel if you don't want to go to a nightclub.

If you like dancing, you'll really enjoy the nightclub.

If you have children, we'll arrange a nanny to look after them.

If you want to do some shopping, you'll have time to go to the shops on Saturday.

4.2

-an endings		-ish endings	
America	American	England	English
Hungary	Hungarian	Turkey	Turkish
Germany	German	Scotland	Scottish
Italy	Italian	Ireland	Irish
Argentina	Argentinian	Poland	Polish
Belgium	Belgian	Denmark	Danish
Morocco	Moroccan	Spain	Spanish
Russia	Russian		
Norway	Norwegian		
Egypt	Egyptian		
Austria	Austrian		
Brazil	Brazilian		
Mexico	Mexican		
Korea	Korean		

-ese endings		-i endings	
Japan	Japanese	Iraq	Iraqi
Portugal	Portuguese	Israel	Israeli
China	Chinese	Pakistan	Pakistani

Irregular

France	French
the Netherlands	Dutch
Thailand	Thai
Greece	Greek

4.3

Hello, Waterman International. Mr Waterman's office. I'm afraid there's nobody in the office at the moment, but if you leave your name and number, Mr Waterman will get back to you as soon as possible. Please speak after the tone. Thank you.

Peter Oh, hi, Jack. This is Peter here. Look, I'm phoning about the results of that Dutch project. They look interesting. Anyway, I'll put them in the post. OK? Bye.

Wife Hello, darling. I'm afraid I'm still in France. My meeting is taking longer than I expected. I probably won't be back till tomorrow. But I'm sure you'll be OK without me for just one more night. Anyway, I'll give you a ring this evening. Will you be in? I'll try about bedtime. Bye.

Sarah Jones Hello, Mr Waterman. This is Sarah Jones. I'm afraid I'm stuck in a traffic jam on the M25, so I probably won't be there till about half past two. I hope that won't be too late. I'll give you the number of my mobile in case you want to call me back. It's 0860 639270. Thank you. Goodbye.

Dennis Jack? Dennis. I'm just returning your call. I'm working at home this afternoon, so can you phone me there? That's 577 9898.

Mother Oh, er Jack, dear. Oh, it's your mother, erm er I, oh, I hate these silly machines. I, oh it doesn't matter.

Teresa Hello, Jack. This is Teresa. I just wanted to talk to you about the new adverts. As you're not there, I'll have a chat with the agency this morning. Should be interesting. I'm off to the

States today for a week, so I'll drop you a line before I go. And I'll be in touch when I get back. Bye.

Son Yo, Dad. I'm going out now and then we're going to a party tonight. So I don't know when I'll be back. (Hey, stop it, look I'm talking to my dad here.) Sorry about that, Dad. Anyway, look, I'm just ringing to say, will it be all right if I take the car? Thanks, Dad.

4.8

Part 1

The train crossed into Bulgaria at two o'clock in the morning. Then it stopped and suddenly there were a lot of policemen on the train.

'What's happening?' I said in Italian to the old man next to me.

'I don't know,' he said.

Then two policemen came into our carriage, a tall thin one and a short fat one. They looked at everybody carefully … and then they looked at me again.

'Come with us, please,' the fat policeman said in English.

'What? Me?' I said. 'Why? What's the matter?'

'Is this your bag?' the tall policeman asked.

I began to ask a question, but policemen never like questions from young men. So I stayed quiet and went with them.

In the station building there were a lot more policemen, and some people from the train. They were all young people, I saw. Some were afraid, some were bored. The police looked in everybody's bags, and then the people went back to the train.

My two policemen took me to a table. 'Your passport, please,' the fat policeman said, 'and open your bag.'

They looked at my passport and began to look through my bag.

'Aha!' the tall policeman said suddenly. All my dirty shirts and clothes were out on the table.

Part 2

The policeman picked up my bag and turned it over. Onto the table, out of my bag, fell packet after packet of American dollars. Nice, new dollars. Fifty dollar notes in big packets. A lot of money.

My mouth opened, and stayed open.

'50,000 … 100,000 … 150,000 … there's 200,000 dollars here,' the tall policeman said. 'What an interesting bag, Mr Tom Walsh.'

'But it's not my bag!' I shouted.

There was a big happy smile on that policeman's face. 'Well,' he said, 'it's got your name on it. Look!' So I looked, and of course there was my name, and yes, of course it was my bag. So how did 200,000 American dollars get into my bag?

'You cannot bring US dollars into the country,' the fat policeman said.

'But I didn't bring them,' I said quickly. 'They're not my dollars. I never saw them before in my life, and–'

There was a lot of noise in the station. I looked out of the window and saw my train. Slowly, it began to move.

'Hey!' I shouted, 'that's my train–'

The tall policeman laughed.

'Oh no,' he said. 'You're not getting back on that train. You're staying here with us, in our beautiful country,' he smiled, happily.

Part 3

So I never got to Sofia on Saturday. I was very unhappy about that. I wanted to have a little talk with Melanie and Carol, ask them one or two questions, you know. *You're a nice guy, Tom. See you in Sofia, OK? Take you to the best restaurant in town.* Yeah. Great.

And I never got down to Cyprus or North Africa that winter. Oh well, you live and learn. It's not an easy life in prison. But it's warm in winter, and the food's not bad. And I'm meeting some interesting people. There's a man from Georgia – Boris, his name is. He comes from a place by the Black Sea. He's a great guy. When we get out of here, he and I are going down to Australia … Brisbane perhaps, or Sydney. Get a job on a ship, start a new life. Yeah, next year will be OK.

5.1

1 Lead is heavier than iron, but gold is the heaviest.

2 The Earth is further from the Sun than Venus, but Mars is the furthest.

3 Christianity is an older religion than Islam, but Buddhism is the oldest.

4 Canada is bigger than China, but Russia is the biggest.

5 A jet engine is more powerful than a diesel engine, but a rocket engine is the most powerful.

6 Rio de Janeiro is closer to the equator than Cairo, but Singapore is the closest.

5.2

1 Which is the highest mountain in the world? *Mount Everest*

2 Which is the biggest island in the world? *Greenland*

3 Which elephant has bigger ears, the African or the Indian elephant? *the African*

4 Which country has the largest population in the world? *China*

5 Which animal is faster, a cheetah or a lion? *a cheetah*

6 Which is the most ancient monument in the world? *the Pyramids*

7 Which is the most intelligent animal in the world? *Apart from human beings, the chimpanzee, but whales, dolphins and orang-utans are also very intelligent.*

5.3

Who are the best drivers? Which drivers are the safest on the roads? According to a recent survey, young and inexperienced drivers are the most likely to have an accident. Older drivers are more careful. Gender makes a difference, too. Young men have the worst accident records of all. They are generally more aggressive than older drivers. They also choose faster cars with bigger engines. One of the most interesting facts in the survey is that passengers have an effect on the driver. When young male drivers have their friends in the car, their driving becomes worse. When their wife or girlfriend is in the car, however, their driving is better. But the opposite is true for women. Their driving is more dangerous when their husband or boyfriend is in the car!

5.4

Assistant Can I help you?

Customer Yes, how much are these T-shirts?

Assistant They're £12.50 each.

Customer I like this one, but it isn't big enough. Have you got it in a larger size?

Assistant Just a minute. No, I'm sorry, we haven't. What about the black one?

Customer No, it's too dark. I'd prefer something lighter.

Assistant How about this blue one?

Customer Yes, that's nice. I'll take it.

Assistant Anything else?

Customer No, that's all, thank you.

Assistant That's £12.50 then, please.

Customer Here you are.

Assistant   Thank you. That's £7.50 change.
Customer   Thank you. Goodbye.

5.5

1 **Customer**   How much is this jacket?
  Assistant   It's £62.
  Customer   Have you got it in brown?
  Assistant   Let me see. Yes, here you are.
  Customer   Yes, yes, that looks fine. I'll take it.
  Assistant   Thank you. Anything else?
  Customer   No, thank you, that's all.
2 **Assistant**   Can I help you?
  Customer   Oh, no, thank you. I'm only looking.
  Assistant   OK. Let me know if you need any help.
  Customer   Thank you.
3 **Assistant**   Can I help you?
  Customer   Yes, I'd like to try these shoes in a size 4, please.
  Assistant   Yes, just a moment. … I'm sorry but we've only got them in a four and a half. Do you want to try them on?
  Customer   Erm, yes, all right. … No, I'm afraid they're too big.
  Assistant   Would you like to try anything else?
  Customer   No, I'll leave it. Thanks anyway.
  Assistant   Thank you.
4 **Customer**   Excuse me. Could I try these jeans on, please?
  Assistant   Certainly. The changing rooms are over there.
  Customer   Thank you.
  Assistant   Are they all right?
  Customer   No, I'm afraid they're too tight. Have you got them in a larger size?
  Assistant   Yes, here you are.
  Customer   Thank you.
  Assistant   Are they any better?
  Customer   Yes, they're fine. I'll take them. How much are they?
  Assistant   They're £34.
5 **Customer**   Could I have this jumper, please?
  Assistant   Certainly. Anything else?
  Customer   Yes, have you got any grey tights?
  Assistant   Are these OK?
  Customer   No, they aren't dark enough.
  Assistant   What about these?
  Customer   Oh yes, they'll be fine.
  Assistant   Is that all?
  Customer   Yes, thank you.
  Assistant   Well, that's £22.90 altogether then, please.

5.8

You've got what it takes

You don't drive a big, fast car.
You don't look like a movie star.
And on your money we won't get far.
But baby,
You've got what it takes
To satisfy.
You've got what it takes
To set my soul on fire.
Whoa, whoa, whoa, whoa, whoa yeah
You've got what it takes for me.
Now you don't live in a beautiful place.
And you don't dress in the best of taste.
And nature didn't give you such a beautiful face.
But baby,
You've got what it takes…
Now when you're near me
Oo-ee
My head goes round and round.
And when you kiss me
Oo-ee
My love comes tumbling down.
You send me.

6.1

One afternoon I went upstairs to have a bath. As I was getting into the bath, the telephone rang in the hall. I was expecting an important call, so I ran downstairs. There was nobody else at home, so I didn't get dressed again. However, while I was standing in the hall with nothing on, I heard voices outside the front door. It was my teenage daughter and her friends, but I couldn't get back upstairs in time. I put down the phone, ran into the living room and hid behind the curtains. Unfortunately, the window cleaner was cleaning the living room windows. When I suddenly appeared, the poor man fell off his ladder. Fortunately, when my daughter and her friends heard the noise, they ran outside. When I looked out of the window, they were helping the window cleaner. So I went upstairs and put on a dressing gown. Luckily the window cleaner wasn't hurt, but it was all very embarrassing.

6.2

Conversation 1

Tourist   Excuse me. Could you tell me how to get to the station, please?
Passer-by   The station. Let me see … Oh yes. Go down this road. Take the second, no, the third turning on the left. That's Canning Street.
Tourist   Canning Street?
Passer-by   Yes. Go along Canning Street and carry on until you come to the second set of traffic lights. Turn right there and you'll see a bridge in front of you. Don't go under the bridge. The station is on the left just before it.
Tourist   So that's down here and take the third turning on the left.
Passer-by   Yes, then carry on along there …
Tourist   Till I come to some traffic lights.
Passer-by   To the second set of traffic lights. It's a big crossroads and there's a BP garage on the corner. You can't miss it.
Tourist   So to the second set of traffic lights, then turn right?
Passer-by   Yes, turn right and the entrance to the station is just before the bridge – between the bridge and the garage, in fact.
Tourist   And how far is it?
Passer-by   Oh, it's a good ten minutes' walk.
Tourist   Thank you.

Conversation 2

Tourist   Excuse me. Can you tell me where the George Hotel is?
First passer-by   No, I'm sorry, love. I'm a stranger here myself.
Tourist   Excuse me. Do you know where the George Hotel is?
Second passer-by   The George? Yes, of course. It's in Carlton Square opposite the clock tower.
Tourist   How do I get there?
Second passer-by   Oh, it's quite easy to find. Turn left here just past the zebra crossing. Then go straight on for about a hundred yards and you'll come to Carlton Square on your right. When you turn into the square, you'll see the clock tower, and the George Hotel is on the right next to the post office.
Tourist   Thank you very much.
Second passer-by   Oh, not at all. I think the hotel car park is behind the hotel, by the way.
Tourist   Oh, thank you.

6.5

Presenter   In this week's edition of *It was a normal day* we hear stories from Robin, Katherine and David. They tell us about normal days which became very unusual days. First Robin's story.

Robin   It was nearly ten years ago, so I was about 22. I was working as a builder at the time and I was also the singer with a band in my free time. Anyway, we were building some houses near Farnham in Surrey. It was about half past ten in the morning and most of the other men were having their tea break. They were listening to the radio. I was working on the roof of one of the houses. There was another guy near me. He was painting the windows of the next house. Well, as I said, I sang with a band in my free time and we'd made a record, called *Wild One*. None of the other guys at work knew about it. Anyway, it came on the radio. The man painting the windows said, 'Great. I think this record's stunning. If it doesn't reach number one, I'll eat my paint brush.' I felt very excited when he said that, but I didn't say anything. But then when the record finished the DJ came on and said, 'There, straight into the charts this week at number 11 is *Wild One*'.
Presenter   And what did you do?
Robin   Well, that was enough for me. I climbed down the ladder. I gave my bag of tools to the other guys and said, 'Here, you can have these. I'm off.' And I left. Two weeks later our record hit number one and we had several more hits after that.
Presenter   So a normal day became the start of an exciting new life for Robin. For Katherine it was also the start of a new life, but …
Katherine   Oh yes, it was a normal day – a very normal day. That was the problem. It was two years ago now – about eight o'clock in the evening.
Presenter   What were you doing?
Katherine   We were sitting in the living room. My husband was sitting in an armchair. He was reading the paper, as he always did. I was sitting on the sofa. I was knitting. Our daughter was expecting a baby, you see – our first grandchild – and I was knitting a little cardigan for it. Yellow, it was. There was a quiz show on the TV. It was *Strike it Lucky*. Isn't it interesting how you remember these details? But we weren't really watching it.
Presenter   And what happened?
Katherine   Well, as I said, we were just having a normal evening at home, when suddenly my husband put down his newspaper and said, 'I'm sorry, but I can't stand this any longer. I'm totally bored with our marriage. I don't love you and I want a divorce.'
Presenter   How did you feel?
Katherine   Well, I was stunned. I didn't know what to think or feel.
Presenter   What did you do?
Katherine   I didn't do anything. It's funny but I just carried on with the cardigan. But my husband went upstairs and packed a suitcase. When he came downstairs I was still knitting. I just couldn't believe what was happening. He said, 'I'm leaving,' and I said, 'Would you like a cup of tea first?' I don't know why I said that. It just came out automatically. Anyway, he just said, 'Oh my God! Is that all you can say?' I wanted to talk about it, but he wasn't interested. He just picked up his suitcase and left.
Presenter   Finally we come to David's story. David is a bank manager.
David   Oh yes, I can remember it as if it was yesterday. I was at work at the time – at the bank. I was having a meeting with my staff. We were all sitting around the big table in my office. It was a rather boring meeting, but most meetings are, I suppose. Anyway, while Sarah

135

Harvey, the assistant manager, was speaking, my secretary came in and said, 'There's a phone call for you.' Well, normally my secretary doesn't interrupt meetings for phone calls. She takes a message. So I was surprised when she came in. 'It's your wife,' she said. 'She says it's urgent.' I was rather worried at this. My wife doesn't panic easily.

Presenter What did you do?

David I went into the secretary's office and I picked up the phone. My wife answered, but immediately a man's voice came on the line. He said, 'We've got your wife and children here. Listen and follow my instructions and they'll be all right.' I was shocked, but I listened to the instructions. 'In ten minutes' time,' he said, 'a man in a green jumper will come into your bank. Give him all the money from the safe. When he telephones me, we'll release your family.' And then he put the phone down.

Presenter What did you do?

David Well, I just did as he said. I had no choice. It was very worrying at the time, but everyone was all right in the end. The police found some of the money, but they never caught the men.

7.2

Martin Hello. Inge Lindstrom?

Inge Yes.

Martin I'm Martin Clay. I'm sorry I'm a bit late. Have you been here long?

Inge No, just a few minutes. The plane was early.

Martin Did you have a good flight?

Inge Yes, it was fine, thanks.

Martin Well, I've parked in the multi-storey, so we need to take the lift over there. Here, let me take your suitcase.

Inge Thank you.

Martin Have you ever been to Manchester before?

Inge No, I've been to London, but this is my first visit to the north of England.

Martin So you haven't seen the real England yet?

Inge 'The real England'? Oh, no, I haven't, just London.

Martin When were you in London?

Inge About three years ago now.

Martin Was that on business?

Inge No, it was a holiday.

Martin Oh, I see. Now, have you eaten?

Inge I had something on the plane, but it wasn't very good, so I didn't eat much.

Martin OK, well I've booked you into the Park Hotel. So I'll drop you there. Then I'll come back in about half an hour and we can go for a meal.

Inge That sounds fine. Thank you.

Martin Is everything OK with your room?

Inge Yes, thank you.

Martin OK, well, now what about something to eat? Have you ever tried Indian food?

Inge No, I haven't.

Martin Well it's very hot, you know, spicy. Do you like hot food?

Inge I'm not sure, but I'll give it a try …

Martin Good. There's a new Indian restaurant near here. I tried it a couple of weeks ago and it's very good. It's called the Bombay.

Martin How was the meal?

Inge Delicious. But you were right. It was very hot.

Martin Well, not too hot, I hope. Erm, have you seen the programme for your visit?

Inge Yes, I received a copy last week, but I've left it at the hotel.

Martin That's OK. I've got another one here. I haven't planned anything for the weekend yet. What would you like to do?

Inge I haven't really thought about it.

Martin Have you heard of the Lake District?

Inge Oh yes. I've always wanted to go there. We studied William Wordsworth's poems at school.

Martin Right, well we'll try the lakes on Saturday then. What about …

7.5

When he left school, Maximilian also started work on the family farm. But he soon became bored. Country life wasn't for him. And so at the age of 18 he left the village. He's only been back three times since then. He went to Buenos Aires and there he got a job on a ship that was sailing to the USA. On the ship he met a rich American businessman. He liked Maximilian and offered him a job. Maximilian learnt quickly and in the next ten years he made a lot of money on Wall Street. He became a millionaire when he was only 25. Since then he has been part of the international jet set. He's had three wives. When he was 30 he married a beautiful model, but she died two years later in a car crash. His second and third marriages both ended in divorce. For the last ten years he has lived alone in his luxury villa in the Bahamas. His family life has not been happy. Two years ago his son went to prison. One of his two daughters has become a drug addict. He's been on television several times and the newspapers have followed his life closely. For the whole of his life he has loved to travel. He's visited almost every country in the world. 'Yes, I've made a lot of money. I've been everywhere and I've done everything. But has it made me happy? Not really. Now look at my brother, Emilio. For seventy years his life hasn't changed at all. But he's happy. Yes, Emilio is a happy man.'

8.3

Waiter Good afternoon.

Customer 1 Have you got a table for two, please?

Waiter This way, please.

Waiter The menu.

Customer 1 Thank you.

Waiter The soup of the day is leek and potato. Would you like an aperitif while you're deciding?

Customer 1 Yes, please. A mineral water for me.

Waiter Still or sparkling?

Customer 1 Sparkling, please.

Customer 2 And I'll have a gin and tonic, please.

Waiter Thank you.

Waiter A mineral water and a gin and tonic. Are you ready to order?

Customer 2 Yes. Could I have the melon and the halibut, please?

Waiter Would you like salad or vegetables, French fries or a jacket potato with the halibut?

Customer 2 Salad and a jacket potato, please.

Customer 1 And I'll have the soup followed by the lamb chops. And I'd like that with salad and French fries, please.

Waiter Thank you. Would you like wine with the meal?

Customer 1 Yes, could we have a bottle of house red, please?

Waiter Thank you.

Waiter The halibut?

Customer 2 Yes. That's for me, please.

Waiter And the lamb chops. Enjoy your meal.

Customer 1 Thank you.

Customer 1 How's the halibut?

Customer 2 Fine. What about your lamb?

Customer 1 Delicious.

Waiter Is everything all right?

Customer 1 Yes, thank you. Could we have two more glasses of mineral water, please?

Waiter Certainly, right away.

Waiter Would you like any dessert?

Customer 1 Well, I'm full. What about you?

Customer 2 Not for me, thanks. But I'd like a cup of coffee.

Customer 1 And I'll have a tea, please.

Waiter So that's one coffee and one tea.

Customer 1 Yes, and could I have the bill, please?

Waiter Did you enjoy your meal?

Customer 1 Yes, thank you. It was very nice. Could I have a receipt for the bill, please?

Waiter Of course. Here you are.

Customer 1 Thank you.

8.7

What do your answers to the questionnaire mean? Write what you must add or subtract in the boxes.

1 If you're a man subtract 3 years and if you're a woman add 4 years.

2 If you're between 30 and 39 years old add 2 years; if you're between 40 and 59 add 3 years; between 50 and 69 add 4 years.

3/4 Towns and cities are unhealthy places. If you live in a large town or city take off 2 years, but if you live in a village or in the country, add 2 years.

5/6 Married people live longer. Take off three years if you live on your own, but you can add 5 years if you live with a partner.

7/8 Education is good for you. Add 1 year for a university degree and another 2 years for a postgraduate qualification.

9 If you sit down most of the day, subtract 3 years.

10 Add 2 years if you exercise for at least 20–30 minutes 3 times a week.

11 If you spend more than 10 hours a day asleep, take off 4 years.

12 If you're happy add a year. If you're unhappy subtract 2 years.

13 If you're relaxed add three years. Subtract three years if you're quick-tempered and aggressive.

14 Don't smoke if you want a long life. Subtract 3 years for up to 10 cigarettes a day, 4 years for 10 to 20, 6 years for up to 40 and 8 years for more than 40. If you're a non-smoker, but you live with a smoker, take off 1 year.

15 Three glasses of wine or beer a day are OK for men, 2 are OK for women. If you drink more than this, take off a year.

16 Overweight? If you're up to 15 kilos too heavy subtract 2 years, 16–25 kilos take off 4 years.

17 Long life runs in families. Add 2 years for each grandparent over 80 years old now or when they died.

18 Some diseases are hereditary, too. Take off three years if anyone in your close family (brothers, sisters, parents, grandparents) has or had heart trouble. Take off another year if anyone in your family died under the age of 50.

To calculate your life expectancy, start with an average age of 72 years. Then add or subtract the numbers.

9.1

How honest are *you*? This is what our psychologist says about the answers.

Question 1: What would you do if you found some money? Give yourself two points for b: *I'd take it to a police station* and one point for c.

Question 2: If somebody tried to sell you a stolen video recorder, would you buy it? Give yourself two points for c and one point for a.

Question 3: If your friend tried to steal something from a shop, what would you do? Two points for c and one for b.

Question 4: If you couldn't afford your car insurance, what would you do? Give yourself two points for a: *the car would stay in the garage until I had enough money.* And one point for c: *I wouldn't drive it except in an emergency.*

Question 5: If a shop assistant gave you too much change, what would you do? Two points for c and one for b.

How did you score? Seven to nine points shows a very honest person. Four to six points is OK – you are about average. Less than four points – well, you're not very honest, are you? And if you scored ten points – you must be joking. You obviously didn't answer this quiz honestly!

Seriously, though, for most people a lot would depend on the circumstances. For example, a lot of people would keep money that they found in the street if it wasn't very much. But if they found a lot of money in a wallet, they would take it to the police station.

And some people would buy stolen goods if they came from a shop or factory, but they wouldn't buy them if they knew they were stolen from someone's house.

📼 9.2

Receptionist   Good evening, sir.

Guest   Good evening. Do you have a reservation in the name of Jones, please?

Receptionist   Just a minute, sir. Yes, here we are. Mr Alan Jones. Would you like a single room or a double, Mr Jones?

Guest   I'd prefer a double, if you've got one.

Receptionist   And how many nights are you staying?

Guest   Three.

Receptionist   Fine. Well, could you just fill in the registration form and sign it at the bottom, please?

Guest   Yes, certainly.

Receptionist   And how do you want to settle the bill?

Guest   By credit card, if that's all right.

Receptionist   Yes, of course. Could I just take an imprint of the card, sir?

Guest   Yes, here you are.

Receptionist   Thank you. And will you require a newspaper and a wake-up call in the morning?

Guest   Yes, I'd like *The Times* and a call at 7.30, please.

Receptionist   7.30. Very good, sir. Here's your key. Your room number is 429. The lift is over there. Do you need any help with your luggage?

Guest   No, thank you. I've only got a small suitcase.

Receptionist   Well, enjoy your stay.

Guest   Thank you.

📼 9.7

Smart shopping. Would it be a good thing? Well, let's consider some of the advantages and disadvantages. The supermarkets think that it would be a good thing. It would be quicker and there would be no queues at the checkouts. They also think that prices would come down, because they wouldn't need checkout assistants. So they would save money. Of course, the checkout assistants wouldn't like that. They'd lose their jobs.

But would the stores really need fewer people? They wouldn't need checkout assistants, but they'd need technicians to look after and repair the machines. And technicians earn more money than checkout assistants. The shops would also need more security guards and they'd need assistants to help customers when there were problems.

What about the shoppers? What would happen if you put something back on the shelves? What would happen if a child put extra things in the trolley or ran the pen over lots of things on the shelves? Would people really trust the computers? You can watch an assistant and you can argue with an assistant, but you can't with a computer. And what would happen

if there was a power cut?

Finally, what about security? The stores believe that the security arches would stop shoplifters. But how would shoppers feel about the arches? If you just forgot to scan something in the trolley, the alarm would ring when you went through the arch. Everyone in the store would look at you. Wouldn't that be a bit embarrassing?

Smart shopping sounds very simple, but would it need smart shoppers?

📼 10.1

Husband   This year, Karen, I'm going to give up smoking. It won't be easy. But I'm not going to touch another cigarette.

Wife   You won't give up. You make a resolution every year, but you never keep it.

Friend   I know, I'll give up, too. Then we can keep an eye on each other.

Husband   Great idea, John.

Wife   Hmm.

February

Husband   It's all right. We won't have any more.

Friend   Mm, no, we won't …

A year later

Wife   Happy New Year, Mike. Are you going to break your New Year's resolution again this year?

Husband   No, this year I'm going to keep it.

Wife   And why is this year different?

Husband   Because this year I'm going to stop making New Year's resolutions!

📼 10.2

My husband's going to go on a diet.
He isn't going to drink so much beer.
I'm going to take more exercise.
I'm not going to work so hard.
My son's going to have a haircut.
He isn't going to watch so much TV.
My daughter's going to tidy her bedroom.
She isn't going to talk on the phone for hours.
We're going to be nicer to each other.
We aren't going to argue with each other.

📼 10.3

How many calories can you burn in one hour? Well, it all depends on the activity.

You use calories all the time, even when you are resting. Reading, sleeping, sitting and sunbathing all use about 60 calories an hour.

Very light activities use 75 calories. Examples are eating, writing, knitting, shaving, driving and washing up.

Light activities which use about 100 calories an hour include playing the piano, getting dressed and having a shower.

Under moderate activities which use between 100 and 200 calories an hour we can put walking, doing housework, shopping and skating.

Energetic activities use 200–400 calories. These include horse riding, cycling, swimming, skipping and dancing.

Finally there are strenuous activities which use up to 600 calories an hour. These activities include climbing stairs, jogging, digging the garden and playing football.

📼 10.4

1 **A**   What are we going to do today?

   B   I don't know. Do you fancy going to the beach?

   A   No, not really. I don't think it's warm enough. But we could go for a picnic in the country.

   B   Yes, that's a good idea. Where shall we go?

   A   Why don't we go to that place by the river? You know, we went there with your friend from Spain.

   B   Oh, yes, that'll be nice. And how about inviting Diane and Peter?

   A   Sure. Do you think you could give them a ring? I'll get some things ready.

   B   OK.

2 **A**   Let's go out for a meal tonight.

   B   OK. Where?

   A   The Red Dragon?

   B   Mmm. We went there last time. I'd rather try somewhere different.

   A   Well, what about trying that new Italian place near the station – what's it called?

   B   Mario's. Yes, people say it's pretty good. Shall I book a table for nine o'clock?

   A   It's all right, I don't mind doing it. Could you pass the phone book?

   B   Here you are.

   A   Thanks.

3 **A**   Would you like to go to the cinema tonight?

   B   No, I don't fancy going out. I'm a bit tired.

   A   Oh, OK. Well, why don't we hire a video?

   B   Yes, OK, but would you mind going to get it? I'm just going to have a bath.

   A   No, I don't mind. I enjoy seeing what they've got. What do you fancy?

   B   Oh anything – but nothing too serious. And why don't you bring a couple of pizzas back with you?

   A   Good idea. OK, see you later.

📼 10.9

Interviewer   'Pleasure is the beginning and the end of living happily.' Those are the words of the Greek philosopher Epicurus, who lived 2,300 years ago. People have always tried to find pleasure and today we have many more pleasures than the Ancient Greeks had. And yet we still don't know a lot about this important part of life. Here in the studio is Dr Jonathan Shamberg. Good evening, Dr Shamberg.

Dr Shamberg   Good evening. It's a pleasure to be here.

Interviewer   Yes, indeed. Well, what things give people most pleasure?

Dr Shamberg   We don't all enjoy the same things. Pleasure means different things to different people. Some people get pleasure from jumping out of aeroplanes or driving at 200 kph. For others pleasure comes from relaxing in a hot bath or playing with children. Doing a crossword or repairing the car give other people pleasure.

Interviewer   What's the purpose of pleasure? Why does it exist?

Dr Shamberg   Well, if pleasure didn't exist, we wouldn't exist. Pleasure is important for human survival. If we want to survive, we have to do three things – eat, have children, and get on with each other. If these things give pleasure, we want to do them. So we survive. That's why we get so much pleasure from food, being in love, and socializing.

Interviewer   But what is pleasure?

Dr Shamberg   Pleasure is a chemical reaction in the brain. When we do something that we enjoy, endorphins and noradrenaline are produced. These stimulate pleasure centres in the brain.

Interviewer   And is pleasure good for you?

Dr Shamberg   Oh yes. The happier you are the longer you will live. But it isn't the great moments of pleasure that are important. Happy people enjoy the ordinary everyday things of life, like cooking a meal, going for a walk or chatting with a friend.

Interviewer   I see. Well, let's talk some more about your research into pleasure …

▣ 10.10

California dreaming

All the leaves are brown,
And the sky is grey.
I've been for a walk
On a winter's day.
I'd be safe and warm
If I was in LA.
California dreaming
On such a winter's day.

Stopped into a church
I passed along the way.
Well, I got down on my knees
And I began to pray.
You know the preacher likes the cold.
He knows I'm gonna stay.
California dreaming
On such a winter's day.

All the leaves are brown,
And the sky is grey.
I've been for a walk
On a winter's day.
If I didn't tell her
I could leave today.
California dreaming
On such a winter's day.

▣ 11.1

Presenter The latest pictures of a member of the royal family have shocked many people. The photographer was Jason Saul. He's a member of the paparazzi and he's with me now. How did you get these photographs?

Jason Saul It wasn't easy. I couldn't get close to the house, so I had to use a very long lens. I was hiding in a tree. I could see the whole house from there but it wasn't very comfortable and it was cold, too.

Presenter How long did you have to wait?

Jason Saul Only a couple of days. For other photos I've had to wait for several days, but this time I was lucky.

Presenter Some people say that you shouldn't do this, because it isn't fair to the royal family.

Jason Saul It's part of public life. If you enjoy the good things, you have to accept the problems. And if you don't want photos like this in the magazines, you have to be more careful. They didn't have to do it by the window.

Presenter Are you going to try to get more photos?

Jason Saul Well, I won't be able to use the same tree again. They've chopped it down. So I'll have to find somewhere else. Or maybe I'll use the money from these photos to buy a longer lens. Then I'll be able to take pictures from further away and I won't have to sit in an uncomfortable tree.

▣ 11.2

Ray Porter Oh, I must phone Kathy Seaton and tell her that I'm going to be in London next week. Now where's the number? Ah, here we are – Nuffield Electronics, 0171 453 8972.

Telephonist Good morning. Nuffield Electronics. My name's Tracy. How may I help you?

Ray Porter Oh, good morning. Could I have extension 233, please?

Telephonist One moment, please. I'm sorry, caller, there's no reply.

Ray Porter Oh, OK. I'll try again later.

Ray Porter Well, let's try Kathy again.

Telephonist Good afternoon. Nuffield Electronics. My name's Tracy. How may I help you?

Ray Porter Could I speak to Kathy Seaton, please?

Telephonist One moment, please. I'm sorry, the line's engaged. Would you like to hold?

Ray Porter Yes, OK. I'll hang on.

Telephonist I'm sorry to keep you. I'm afraid the line's still busy.

Ray Porter Well, can I leave a message for her?

Telephonist Just one moment, please. I'm just putting you through to her secretary.

Man Hello, Sales Department.

Ray Porter Hello. Could I leave a message for Kathy Seaton, please?

Man I'm sorry. I think you've got the wrong extension. Just one moment, please.

Telephonist Hello. Switchboard.

Man Could you transfer this call to Kathy Seaton, please?

Telephonist Right, I'm just putting you through now.

Secretary Hello, extension 233, Kathy Seaton's office.

Ray Porter Hello. My name's Ray Porter. Could I leave a message for Kathy, please?

Secretary Certainly, Mr Porter.

Ray Porter Could you tell her that I'm going to be in London next Tuesday? Can we get together for a meal?

Secretary Oh, I'm sorry, Mr Porter, but Mrs Seaton is going to be in Japan all next week. Mr Porter? Mr Porter? Strange. He's hung up.

▣ 11.6

1 Woman The most difficult event for me was the Wall. We had to climb this huge wall. It's over 10 metres high. That was bad enough, but then after 10 seconds two of the Gladiators followed us up the wall. They had to try and pull us off the wall before we got to the top. Scorpio was chasing me and Jet was chasing the other contender. I told myself: don't look down. I knew that if I looked down and saw Scorpio, that would be the end. So I had to climb and climb and ignore this Gladiator behind me. But I did it. I reached the top of the wall and I got ten points for that. The other girl wasn't so lucky. Jet caught her and pulled her off the wall.

2 Man I remember Hang Tough the best. I was against Saracen. He's really good at this event. In Hang Tough there's a platform each side of the arena. I was on one and Saracen was on the other one. Between us there were sixty rings – about 12 feet off the ground. Anyway I had to swing across the arena and get to Saracen's platform. He had to try and stop me. Well, I was about halfway across when he caught me. He put his legs round me, but he didn't pull me down. I hung on for the whole minute and so I scored five points. That was the longest minute of my whole life and I'm sure my arms were longer afterwards. But I did it. I scored five points against Saracen. And that felt really great!

3 Man Ah yes! Duel. That was the shortest event for me. I was on a platform and Trojan was on another platform. Now Trojan is big, and I mean big with a capital B. Well, we both had a big stick – called a pugil stick – and we had to knock each other off the platform or stay on the platform for 60 seconds. 60 seconds! I didn't last six seconds. Trojan swung his stick and *whoompf* I was on the floor. Incredible.

▣ 12.1

In 1973 a 75-tonne space station called *Skylab* was launched by the USA. Three crews of three astronauts were sent to *Skylab*, but at the end of 1974, it was abandoned. *Skylab* stayed in space until 1979. Then it fell out of its orbit and headed towards the Earth. A lot of the space station burnt up when it entered the atmosphere. But not all of it was destroyed. Large pieces were scattered across the Indian Ocean. Australia was hit by some fragments. Fortunately nobody was hurt. A lot of the pieces were found by Australian farmers. The pieces were sold for very high prices.

▣ 12.2

1 **A** Peter and I are getting married.
  B Congratulations! When's the happy day?
2 **A** I've got an interview for a job today.
  B Good luck! I'll keep my fingers crossed for you.
3 **A** John can't play today. It seems he's had an accident.
  B Oh dear. It's nothing serious, I hope.
4 **A** Did you know Tony and Rosie have split up?
  B Oh, really? When did that happen?
5 **A** I won the gold medal in the race.
  B Well done! I knew you could do it.
6 **A** I'm expecting a baby.
  B That's wonderful news! When's it due?
7 **A** I'm afraid I failed my driving test.
  B Oh well, never mind. Better luck next time!
8 **A** Have you heard? Sue had her baby on Saturday.
  B Oh wonderful! Was it a boy or a girl?
9 **A** Happy Birthday, Mummy!
  B Thank you very much. How sweet of you.

▣ 12.5

Pure gold is rare. It's been used for over 6,000 years, but there are still only about 110,000 tons in the world. It is usually mixed with other metals. The proportion of gold is shown in carats. Pure gold is 24 carat and the cheapest is 9 carat. The word *carat* comes from the Greek word, *keration*, which means a carob seed. These seeds were used to weigh gold and diamonds.

Most gold today is found in South Africa (612 tons a year) and North America (459 tons a year). About 83% of it is used for jewellery. Of the rest about 9% is used by industry, about 6% is used for coins and 2% is made into gold teeth. Gold is usually found in very small pieces or 'nuggets'. The largest nugget, the Holtermann Nugget, was found in 1872 in Australia. It weighed 214 kilograms.

The largest reserves of gold are held in the USA in the Federal Reserve Bank and Fort Knox. The second biggest stores are held by the Bank of England and the Bank of France. Not all of this gold belongs to the governments of these countries. A lot of it is owned by companies, other governments, and individuals. When gold is bought and sold, it isn't usually moved. Only the names on a piece of paper are changed. The gold itself stays in the bank.

The first gold coins were used in Turkey in 670 BC. But gold has always been accepted as money anywhere in the world. Sailors, for example, used to wear a gold earring. If they were shipwrecked, they could pay to get home again. Gold is still given to military pilots for the same reason.

People have always been fascinated by gold. How many crimes have been committed and how many lives have been lost for it? The gold of the Pharaohs was stolen from their tombs in the Pyramids. The Inca and Aztec empires were destroyed for gold. Hundreds of men died in the jungles of South America as they searched for the golden city of Eldorado. In 1849 thousands of people left their homes to join the California Gold Rush. Many were killed by Indians, outlaws and disease.

▣ 13.1

Well, let's see. In 1973, I'd finished school, but I hadn't left home by then. I'd seen the Beatles of course – on the TV and in concert, too. And my hair was still lovely and fair. It hadn't turned grey!

I'd had a boyfriend, too. We used to go dancing. I'd started work by then – in a film laboratory. I hadn't heard of Margaret Thatcher, of course. I was so surprised to hear about a woman prime minister. I hadn't been abroad, either. I hadn't been anywhere! I'd had a favourite pop group. They were called T. Rex. I was so sad to hear that the lead singer had died. I hadn't used a personal computer, of course. They hadn't been invented!

📖 13.2

1 Customer Hello. Could you give me some information about flight times to Istanbul, please?

Clerk When do you want to travel?

Customer I want to leave on 22 November and return on December 3.

Clerk Well, on the 22nd there's a flight at 12.25. That gets to Istanbul at 16.40.

Customer Hmm. That's a bit late.

Clerk Well, there's an evening flight on the 21st at 18.05. It arrives in Istanbul at 22.30.

Customer I see. What about the return flight?

Clerk Yes, what was the date again?

Customer 3 December.

Clerk There's a flight at 8.30 in the morning. That arrives at 12.50.

Customer OK. Well, can I book the flights on the 21st and the 3rd then, please?

Clerk Certainly. What name is it, please?

2 Customer Hello. Have you got any seats available on March 12 or April 5?

Clerk Let me see. No. I'm afraid 12 March is fully booked, and 5 April is fully booked, too.

Customer Oh dear.

Clerk We have some seats available on 10 May or 17 May. Otherwise it's June or July.

Customer No, well, I think 10 May is OK.

Clerk How many seats do you need?

Customer Three.

Clerk Well, we've got three seats in Row J …

3 Clerk Hello. Can I help you?

Customer Yes, I've got an appointment with Doctor Clark on 26 August, but I'm afraid I can't make it. Can I change it to another date, please?

Clerk Hmm. Well, there's nothing left in August now.

Customer That's all right. It's only for a check-up.

Clerk Can you come on 8 September at 3.30?

Customer Yes, that's fine.

Clerk What name is it, please?

📖 13.6

The strange story of Martin Guerre

It was 1538 and in the village of Artigat in south-west France there was a wedding. The bride was Bertrande de Rols and the bridegroom was Martin Guerre. They didn't love each other. The marriage had been arranged by Martin's father, Sangxi, in order to unite the two richest families in the village. The marriage was not a happy one. Martin was a tall and strong young man, but he was lazy and bad-tempered, and he treated Bertrande very badly. Martin had half of the family's farm. Sangxi's brother, Pierre, had the other half. But while Pierre worked hard on his part of the farm, Martin spent all his time with his friends in the village.

One day Sangxi caught his son in the barn. He was stealing some of Pierre's produce. Sangxi was furious, so the next day Martin secretly left the village. The family waited for news, but none came. Martin Guerre had simply disappeared. Only Sangxi knew why.

Then, eight years later, Martin suddenly returned. He had changed a lot while he had been away. In fact,

he was like a new man. He was pleasant and helpful, and treated Bertrande well. He also worked hard on the farm. Bertrande and Martin now lived happily together and they soon had a daughter. Their happy life did not last long, however. While Martin had been away, Sangxi had died, and because Martin had disappeared, Pierre had inherited everything. Now that Martin had returned, Pierre would have to give him half of the inheritance – £7,000. Pierre and Martin argued about the money for three years.

Then one day Pierre received some strange information. Someone said that he had seen Martin Guerre in Flanders. The village shoemaker was also sure that Martin's shoes were now three sizes smaller than before he had left. This was Pierre's chance. He went to court and claimed that this new Martin was not the real Martin Guerre.

At the trial some people (including Martin's four sisters) said that the new Martin was the real Martin, but other people said that he wasn't. Finally, the judge decided that he really was Martin. But that was not the end of the story.

📖 13.7

Indeed that was not the end of the story. When the judge at the trial had finally decided that this was the real Martin, a man with a wooden leg came into the court. It was the real Martin Guerre. And then the true story came out.

When Martin had left the village, he had become a soldier in the Spanish army. He had been sent to fight in Flanders. There he had met a man called Arnaud du Tilh. The two men looked very similar. They had become friends and Martin had told Arnaud all about his life in Artigat. Then in a battle Martin Guerre had been wounded in the leg. Arnaud had thought that he would die, so he had decided to take Martin's place and get his money. But then he had fallen in love with Bertrande and had decided to stay.

Martin, however, hadn't died and later he had heard about the trial. And so Martin returned to his home. Bertrande got her lazy and bad-tempered husband back. Pierre lost the £7,000. And as for Arnaud? He was hanged in front of Martin Guerre's house.

📖 14.1

OK, let's take a look at Kate's time log. What did she do in her morning? She arrived at work at 9.00. While she was having a cup of coffee, John came in. They talked about a TV programme that they had watched the night before. At 9.15 Kate went to have a word with Fred about the meeting the next day, but Fred wasn't there, so she walked back to her office.

After she had read the morning's post, she decided to start work. But Amanda phoned. She was back from her holiday. They chatted till 10.30. After the coffee break, Kate started work, but the computer wasn't working, so she phoned the engineer. Then she walked to the computer laboratory, but all the computers were being used, so she returned to the office. The computer engineer had arrived. He explained the problem. Kate started typing a letter at twelve o'clock. At 12.30 she went to lunch.

So what has Kate achieved in her morning's work? In four hours she has really only done two things: she's read the morning's post and she's typed a letter. Not a lot for four hours!

📖 14.2

TMS consultant Now I believe that if you use our time management techniques, you can save yourself at least one hour a day. But there's no point in saving an hour, if you then waste it. So what would you do with that extra hour?

A An extra hour? I'd stay in bed longer. I hate getting up.

B I'd leave work an hour earlier each day and I'd spend more time with my family. Kids grow up so quickly and if you aren't careful you miss it, because you're working all the time.

C I'd get more exercise. I think I'd spend an hour in the gym each day, or swimming maybe. I'd like to be fitter, but I never find the time to do it.

D I'm not sure really. I think I'd read more. I don't get time to read all the things that I should.

📖 14.3

Annette Taxi!

Taxi driver Where to, miss?

Annette The Carling Hotel, please.

Taxi driver Certainly. Have you got any luggage?

Annette Yes, I've got this suitcase.

Taxi driver Right. I'll just see to that. Now where are you staying again, miss?

Annette The Carling Hotel in West Street.

Taxi driver Right … A bit grey today, isn't it?

Annette Pardon?

Taxi driver It's a bit grey today, the weather. It's not very nice. You know. Dull.

Annette Oh, I see. No, it isn't very nice.

Taxi driver Still at least it isn't raining.

Annette Yes, that's true.

Taxi driver Is this your first time here?

Annette No. This is my third visit to Oxford.

Taxi driver Are you here on business or on holiday?

Annette On business, I'm afraid.

Taxi driver How long are you staying?

Annette Oh, just two days.

Taxi driver Well, I hope you aren't in a hurry.

Annette No, I'm not. Why?

Taxi driver Well, the traffic's terrible. This is only my second run today.

Annette Oh, really?

Taxi driver There are just too many vehicles on the road.

Annette Well, I think most cities are the same.

Taxi driver Where are you from, then?

Annette I'm from Belgium.

Taxi driver Oh, yes. Whereabouts?

Annette Near Brussels.

Taxi driver Oh right … Well, here we are. That's £8.25, please, miss.

Annette Here you are. Keep the change.

Taxi driver Thanks a lot, miss.

📖 14.6

Summertime Blues

I'm a-gonna raise a fuss, I'm a-gonna raise a holler,
About working all summer just to try to make a dollar.
Every time I call my baby and try to make a date,
My boss says, 'No dice, son. You gotta work late.'
Sometimes I wonder what I'm a-gonna do,
But there ain't no cure for the Summertime Blues.
Well, my mom and poppa told me, 'Son you gotta make some money,
If you want to use the car to go driving next Sunday.'
Well I didn't go to work, I told the boss I was sick.
'Now you can't use the car, 'cos you didn't work a lick.'
Sometimes I wonder what I'm a-gonna do,
But there ain't no cure for the Summertime Blues.
I'm gonna take two weeks, I'm gonna have a fine vacation.
I'm gonna take my problem to the United Nations.
Well I called my congressman and he said, 'No.
I'd like to help you, son, but you're too young to vote.'
Sometimes I wonder what I'm a-gonna do,
But there ain't no cure for the Summertime Blues.

Getting started

Grammar
chemistry /'kemɪstri/
details /'di:teɪlz/
female /'fi:meɪl/
to forget /fə'get/
insurance /ɪn'ʃʊərəns/
to introduce /ɪntrə'dju:s/
language /'læŋgwɪʤ/
local /'ləʊkl/
male /meɪl/
model /'mɒdl/
occupation /ˌɒkjʊ'peɪʃn/
postcode /'pəʊstkəʊd/
reason /'ri:zn/
surname /'sɜ:neɪm/
vehicle /'vɪəkl/useful /'ju:sfl/

Vocabulary
ceiling /'si:lɪŋ/
coffee table /'kɒfi ˌteɪbl/
cupboard /'kʌbəd/
floor /flɔ:(r)/
lid /lɪd/
mice /maɪs/
pencil sharpener /'pensl ˌʃɑ:pnə(r)/
piano /pɪ'ænəʊ/
plant /plɑ:nt/
sofa /'səʊfə/
toy /tɔɪ/
vase /vɑ:z/
video cassette /'vɪdɪəʊ kə,set/
wall /wɔ:l/
window sill /'wɪndəʊ ˌsɪl/

Unit 1

Grammar
active /'æktɪv/
argument /'ɑːgjʊmənt/
brain /breɪn/
college /'kɒlɪʤ/
different /'dɪfrənt/
downstairs /daʊn'steəz/
energy /'enəʤi/
to hurry /'hʌri/
in peace /ɪn 'pi:s/
loo /lu:/
loud /laʊd/
opposite /'ɒpəzɪt/
programme /'prəʊgræm/
route /ru:t/
routine /ru:'ti:n/
shower /'ʃaʊə(r)/
to switch on /swɪʧ 'ɒn/
to turn up /tɜ:n 'ʌp/
uncreative /ˌʌŋkri:'eɪtɪv/
volume /'vɒlju:m/
without /wɪ'ðaʊt/

Reading
to allow /ə'laʊ/
army /'ɑ:mi/
caravan /'kærəvæn/
CD player /ˌsi:'di: ˌpleɪə(r)/
to complain /kəm'pleɪn/
to decorate /'dekəreɪt/
to dig /dɪg/
dirty /'dɜ:ti/
disappear /dɪsə'pɪə(r)/
fair /feə(r)/
freedom /'fri:dəm/
gypsy /'ʤɪpsi/
jealous /'ʤeləs/
jewellery /'ʤu:əlri/

---

lazy /'leɪzi/
market /'mɑ:kɪt/
middle class /ˌmɪdl 'klɑ:s/
mortgage /'mɔ:gɪʤ/
to prefer /prɪ'fɜ:(r)/
prison /'prɪzən/
rebel /'rebl/
respectable /rɪ'spektəbl/
simple /'sɪmpl/
slave /sleɪv/
society /sə'saɪəti/
summer /'sʌmə(r)/
tax /tæks/
winter /'wɪntə(r)/

Listening
appointment /ə'pɔɪntmənt/
to book /bʊk/
diary /'daɪəri/
meeting /'mi:tɪŋ/
office /'ɒfɪs/
to record /rɪ'kɔ:d/
to reserve /rɪ'zɜ:v/
wake-up call /'weɪk ʌp ˌkɔ:l/

Extension
alcohol /'ælkəhɒl/
approximately /ə'prɒksɪmətli/
average /'ævrɪʤ/
to beat /bi:t/
bike /baɪk/
billion /'bɪlɪən/
to blink /blɪŋk/
to breathe (in) /bri:ð/
earthquake /'ɜ:θkweɪk/
(the) equator /ɪ'kweɪtə(r)/
to increase /ɪŋ'kri:s/
to land /lænd/
league /li:g/
lifetime /'laɪftaɪm/
loaf /ləʊf/
million /'mɪlɪən/
period /'pɪərɪəd/
pint /paɪnt/
population /ˌpɒpjʊ'leɪʃn/
sweat /swet/
to take off /ˌteɪk 'ɒf/
thousand /'θaʊznd/
to serve /sɜ:v/
weapon /'wepən/

Unit 2

Grammar
airport /'eəpɔ:t/
bank clerk /'bæŋk ˌklɑ:k/
briefcase /'bri:fkeɪs/
construction /kən'strʌkʃn/
couple /'kʌpl/
dam /dæm/
department /dɪ'pɑ:tmənt/
departure lounge /dɪ'pɑ:ʧə ˌlaʊnʤ/
exciting /ɪk'saɪtɪŋ/
for example /fər ɪg'zɑ:mpl/
to kiss /kɪs/
to look round /ˌlʊk 'raʊnd/
motorway /'məʊtəweɪ/
on business /ˌɒn 'bɪznɪs/
outdoors /aʊt'dɔ:z/
to run away /ˌrʌn ə'weɪ/
similar /'sɪmɪlə(r)/
to walk away /ˌwɔ:k ə'weɪ/
to waste /weɪst/
to wonder /'wʌndə(r)/

Vocabulary
bald /bɔ:ld/
curly /'kɜ:li/
fair /feə/
slim /slɪm/
wavy /'weɪvi/
well-built /ˌwel 'bɪlt/

Reading
affectionate /ə'fekʃənət/
appearance /ə'pɪərəns/
to bother (with) /'bɒðə/
character /'kærəktə(r)/
companion /kəm'pænɪən/
divorced /dɪ'vɔ:st/
easy-going /ˌi:zi 'gəʊɪŋ/
fax machine /'fæks məˌʃi:n/
hang-gliding /'hæŋ ˌglaɪdɪŋ/
lifestyle /'laɪfstaɪl/
lively /'laɪvli/
lonely /'ləʊnli/
mobile phone /ˌməʊbaɪl 'fəʊn/
outgoing /aʊt'gəʊɪŋ/
partner /'pɑ:tnə(r)/
reliable /rɪ'laɪəbl/
respectable /rɪ'spektəbl/
responsible /rɪ'spɒnsəbl/
(a) sense of humour /ˌsens əv 'hju:mə(r)/
shy /ʃaɪ/
sincere /sɪn'sɪə(r)/
sociable /'səʊʃəbl/
well-off /ˌwel 'ɒf/
widow /'wɪdəʊ/
willing /'wɪlɪŋ/

Listening
darling /'dɑ:lɪŋ/
director /daɪ'rektə(r)/
to discuss /dɪs'kʌs/
exhibition /ˌeksɪ'bɪʃn/
to get together /ˌget tə'geðə(r)/
to give a lecture /ˌgɪv ə 'lekʧə(r)/
to interview /'ɪntəvju:/
to make arrangements /ˌmeɪk ə'reɪnʤmənts/
play (n) /pleɪ/
to rehearse /rɪ'hɜ:s/
sales meeting /'seɪlz ˌmi:tɪŋ/

Extension
to be expecting a baby /bi: ɪk ˌspektɪŋ ə 'beɪbi/
christening /'krɪsnɪŋ/
engaged /ɪŋ'geɪʤd/
fiancé(e) /fɪ'ɒnseɪ/
firm (n) /fɜ:m/
to get married /ˌget 'mærɪd/
grown up /ˌgrəʊn 'ʌp/
I assume /ˌaɪ ə'sju:m/
I suppose /ˌaɪ sə'pəʊz/
in the middle /ɪn ðə 'mɪdl/
nephew /'nefju:/
niece /ni:s/
single /'sɪŋgl/
sweet /swi:t/
wedding /'wedɪŋ/

Unit 3

Grammar
angry /'æŋgri/
apart /ə'pɑ:t/
to apologize /ə'pɒləʤaɪz/
to approve /ə'pru:v/

---

to attack /ə'tæk/
border /'bɔ:də(r)/
bride /braɪd/
to fall in love (with) /ˌfɔ:l ɪn 'lʌv wɪð/
furious /'fjʊərɪəs/
to get rid of /ˌget 'rɪd əv/
(bride)groom /gru:m/
guest /gest/
permission /pə'mɪʃn/
to smile /smaɪl/
stomach /'stʌmək/

Vocabulary
diamond /'daɪəmənd/
fortune /'fɔ:tju:n/
generous /'ʤenərəs/
to inherit /ɪn'herɪt/
mean (adj) /mi:n/
millionaire /ˌmɪlɪə'neə(r)/
property /'prɒpəti/
wealthy /'welθi/

Reading
eventually /ɪ'ventʃʊəli/
financial /faɪ'nænʃl/
genius /'ʤi:nɪəs/
(to get your) revenge /rɪ'venʤ/
to get better /ˌget 'betə(r)/
ground /graʊnd/
to injure /'ɪnʤə(r)/
to invest /ɪn'vest/
knee /ni:/
laundry /'lɔ:ndri/
to own /əʊn/
to refuse /rɪ'fju:z/
to remove /rɪ'mu:v/
soap /səʊp/
(to have a) stroke /strəʊk/
unfortunately /ʌn'fɔ:tʃənətli/
witch /wɪʧ/

Listening
to agree /ə'gri:/
climate /'klaɪmət/
to close down /ˌkləʊz 'daʊn/
(a) couple of /'kʌpəl əv/
difficult /'dɪfɪkəlt/
far away (from) /ˌfɑ:r ə'weɪ/
to follow /'fɒləʊ/
to grow up /ˌgrəʊ 'ʌp/
kid /kɪd/
to move around /ˌmu:v ə'raʊnd/
relatives /'relətɪvz/
secondary school /'sekəndri ˌsku:l/
sunshine /'sʌnʃaɪn/

Extension
annual /'ænjʊəl/
below /bɪ'ləʊ/
campaign /kæm'peɪn/
championship /'tʃæmpɪənʃɪp/
coast /kəʊst/
dangerous /'deɪnʤərəs/
desperately /'desprətli/
to dive /daɪv/
to escape /ɪ'skeɪp/
to float /fləʊt/
huge /hju:ʤ/
to kick /kɪk/
to knock /nɒk/
photographer /fə'tɒgrəfə(r)/
to protect /prə'tekt/
to realize /'rɪəlaɪz/

rope /rəʊp/
scientist /'saɪəntɪst/
shark /ʃɑːk/
spear-fishing /'spɪə ˌfɪʃɪŋ/
stitch /stɪtʃ/
surface /'sɜːfɪs/
to survive /sə'vaɪv/
to swallow /'swɒləʊ/
to tie /taɪ/

Unit 4

Grammar
backstage /ˌbæk'steɪdʒ/
capital city /ˌkæpɪtəl 'sɪti/
casino /kə'siːnəʊ/
champagne /ʃæm'peɪn/
(a) five-course meal
  /ˌfaɪv kɔːs 'miːl/
limousine /lɪmə'ziːn/
nanny /'næni/
nightclub /'naɪtklʌb/
to relax /rɪ'læks/
representative /ˌreprɪ'zentətɪv/
show (n) /ʃəʊ/
star /stɑː(r)/
world-famous /'wɜːld ˌfeɪməs/
winner /'wɪnə(r)/

Reading
advert /'ædvɜːt/
balance /'bæləns/
chauffeur /'ʃəʊfə(r)/
community /kə'mjuːnəti/
to compete (with) /kəm'piːt/
to continue /kən'tɪnjuː/
controls /kən'trəʊlz/
culture /'kʌltʃə(r)/
to demand /dɪ'mɑːnd/
education /ˌedjʊ'keɪʃn/
housekeeper /'haʊskiːpə(r)/
illegal /ɪ'liːgl/
immigration /ˌɪmɪ'greɪʃn/
including /ɪŋ'kluːdɪŋ/
to integrate (into) /'ɪntɪgreɪt/
lawyer /'lɔɪə(r)/
level (n) /'levl/
maid /meɪd/
minority /maɪ'nɒrəti/
newcomer /'njuːkʌmə(r)/
to overtake /ˌəʊvə'teɪk/
politician /ˌpɒlɪ'tɪʃn/
racial /'reɪʃl/
recently /'riːsntli/
strict /strɪkt/
TV channel /ˌtiː'viː ˌtʃænl/

Listening
agency /'eɪdʒənsi/
answerphone /'ɑːnsəfəʊn/
arrangement(s)
  /ə'reɪndʒmənt(s)/
bedtime /'bedtaɪm/
chat /tʃæt/
confidential /ˌkɒnfɪ'denʃl/
in case /ɪŋ 'keɪs/
message /'mesɪdʒ/
project (n) /'prɒdʒekt/
result(s) /rɪ'zʌlts/
(the) post /pəʊst/
tone /təʊn/
traffic jam /'træfɪk ˌdʒæm/

Extension
to check /tʃek/
compartment /kəm'pɑːtmənt/
corridor /'kɒrɪdɔː(r)/

express /ɪk'spres/
guard /gɑːd/
guy /gaɪ/
luggage rack /'lʌgɪdʒ ˌræk/
meal /miːl/
to move on /ˌmuːv 'ɒn/
note /nəʊt/
packet /'pækɪt/
passport /'pɑːspɔːt/
to pick up /ˌpɪk 'ʌp/
platform /'plætfɔːm/
pocket /'pɒkɪt/
restaurant car /'restrɒnt ˌkɑː(r)/
ticket /'tɪkɪt/

Unit 5

Grammar
(to have an) accident
  /'æksɪdənt/
according to /ə'kɔːdɪŋ tə/
aggressive /ə'gresɪv/
Buddhism /'bʊdɪzm/
Christianity /ˌkrɪstɪ'ænəti/
diesel /'diːzəl/
(the) Earth /ɜːθ/
(to have an) effect (on)
  /ɪ'fekt/
engine /'endʒɪn/
fact /fækt/
fine /faɪn/
gold /gəʊld/
inexperienced /ˌɪnɪk'spɪərɪənst/
iron /'aɪən/
Islam /'ɪzlɑːm/
jet /dʒet/
lead (n) /led/
Mars /mɑːz/
record (n) /'rekɔːd/
rocket /'rɒkɪt/
sunny /'sʌni/
survey /'sɜːveɪ/
Venus /'viːnəs/

Reading
ancient /'eɪnʃənt/
brain /breɪn/
cartoon /kɑː'tuːn/
common /'kɒmən/
contact (n) /'kɒntækt/
dramatic /drə'mætɪk/
eye shadow /'aɪ ˌʃædəʊ/
eyebrow /'aɪbraʊ/
eyelash /'aɪlæʃ/
eyelid /'aɪlɪd/
eyesight /'aɪsaɪt/
false /fɒls/
flexible /'fleksəbl/
to focus /'fəʊkəs/
to gaze /geɪz/
image /'ɪmɪdʒ/
intimate /'ɪntɪmət/
iris /'aɪrɪs/
lens /lenz/
lift (n) /lɪft/
make-up /'meɪk ʌp/
muscle /'mʌsəl/
mysterious /mɪ'stɪərɪəs/
nerve /nɜːv/
pupil /'pjuːpəl/
pyramid /'pɪrəmɪd/
to raise /reɪz/
rare /reə(r)/
retina /'retɪnə/
senses /'sensɪz/
sensitive (to) /'sensətɪv/

sunglasses /'sʌnglɑːsɪz/
tough /tʌf/
to threaten /'θretn/
unconscious /ˌʌn'kɒnʃəs/
upside-down /ˌʌpsaɪd 'daʊn/
to wink /wɪŋk/

Vocabulary
blouse /blaʊz/
sandals /'sændlz/
suit /suːt/
sweatshirt /'swetʃɜːt/
swimsuit /'swɪmsuːt/
tights /taɪts/
trainers /'treɪnəz/
waist /weɪst/

Listening
altogether /ˌɔːltə'geðə(r)/
changing rooms /'tʃeɪndʒɪŋ
  ˌrɒmz/
loose /luːs/
size /saɪz/
tight /taɪt/
to try (on) /traɪ/

Extension
broad /brɔːd/
figure /'fɪgə(r)/
movie star /'muːvi ˌstɑː(r)/
(to set) on fire /ˌɒn 'faɪə(r)/
soul /səʊl/
taste (n) /teɪst/
to satisfy /'sætɪsfaɪ/

Unit 6

Grammar
(ice cream) cone /kəʊn/
curtain /'kɜːtn/
dressing gown /'dresɪŋ ˌgaʊn/
embarrassed /ɪm'bærəst/
embarrassing /ɪm'bærəsɪŋ/
to expect /ɪk'spekt/
to fall off /ˌfɔːl 'ɒf/
fortunately /'fɔːtʃənətli/
in hysterics /ˌɪn hɪ'sterɪks/
incident /'ɪnsɪdənt/
ladder /'lædə(r)/
lake /leɪk/
to look out of /'lʊk ˌaʊt əv/
nobody else /ˌnəʊbədɪ 'els/
terribly /'terəbli/
upstairs /ˌʌp'steəz/
window cleaner /'wɪndəʊ
  ˌkliːnə(r)/

Reading
adventurous /əd'ventʃərəs/
afterwards /'ɑːftəwədz/
amazing /ə'meɪzɪŋ/
calm /kɑːm/
colourful /'kʌləfl/
crime /kraɪm/
direct /daɪ'rekt/
en-suite /ˌɒn 'swiːt/
equipment /ɪ'kwɪpmənt/
experience /ɪk'spɪərɪəns/
fascinating /'fæsəneɪtɪŋ/
flight /flaɪt/
guide /gaɪd/
to hoot /huːt/
lake /leɪk/
luggage /'lʌgɪdʒ/
luxury /'lʌkʃəri/
minibus /'mɪnɪbʌs/
monkey /'mʌŋki/
peaceful(ly) /'piːsfəli/

to prepare /prɪ'peə(r)/
rapids /'ræpɪdz/
to recover (from) /rɪ'kʌvə/
scenery /'siːnəri/
sightseeing tour /'saɪtsiːɪŋ
  ˌtʊə(r)/
souvenir /ˌsuːvə'nɪə(r)/
spectacular /spek'tækjʊlə(r)/
temple /'templ/
tent /tent/
tourist /'tʊərɪst/
trek /trek/
wonderful /'wʌndəfl/

Vocabulary
cathedral /kə'θiːdrəl/
clock tower /'klɒk ˌtaʊə(r)/
leisure centre /'leʒə ˌsentə(r)/
library /'laɪbrəri/
main square /ˌmeɪn 'skweə(r)/
stranger (n) /'streɪndʒə(r)/
town hall /ˌtaʊn 'hɔːl/
traffic lights /'træfɪk ˌlaɪts/
zebra crossing /ˌzebrə 'krɒsɪŋ/

Extension
assistant /ə'sɪstənt/
band /bænd/
builder /'bɪldə(r)/
cardigan /'kɑːdɪgən/
to carry on (with) /ˌkærɪ'ɒn/
choice /tʃɔɪs/
grandchild /'græntʃaɪld/
hit (n) /hɪt/
instructions /ɪn'strʌkʃnz/
to interrupt /ˌɪntə'rʌpt/
to knit /nɪt/
marriage /'mærɪdʒ/
paintbrush /'peɪntbrʌʃ/
to panic /'pænɪk/
quiz show /'kwɪz ˌʃəʊ/
to release /rɪ'liːs/
safe (n) /seɪf/
suitcase /'suːtkeɪs/
tea break /'tiː ˌbreɪk/
tool /tuːl/
urgent /'ɜːdʒənt/

Unit 7

Grammar
abroad /ə'brɔːd/
camel /'kæml/
ice hockey /'aɪs ˌhɒki/
measles /'miːzlz/
windsurfing /'wɪndˌsɜːfɪŋ/

Reading
actor /'æktə(r)/
drunk /drʌŋk/
editor /'edɪtə(r)/
enclose /ɪŋ'kləʊz/
flat (n) /flæt/
former /'fɔːmə(r)/
fraud /frɔːd/
to go out together /ˌgəʊ 'aʊt
  tə.geðə(r)/
gossip /'gɒsɪp/
to guess /ges/
honeymoon /'hʌnimuːn/
law /lɔː/
mad(ly) /mæd(li)/
magnificent /mæg'nɪfɪsənt/
temporary /'temprəri/
twins /twɪnz/
view /vjuː/

Listening
conference /'kɒnfərəns/
delicious /dɪ'lɪʃəs/
multi-storey (car park)
  /'mʌlti ˌstɔːri/
poem /'pəʊɪm/
Extension
beyond /bɪ'jɒnd/
businessman /'bɪznɪsmən/
to celebrate /'seləbreɪt/
celebration /ˌselə'breɪʃn/
chance /tʃɑːns/
childhood /'tʃaɪldhʊd/
to dream /driːm/
drug addict /'drʌg ˌædɪkt/
horizon /hə'raɪzn/
jet set /'dʒet ˌset/
to offer /'ɒfə(r)/
sweetheart /'swiːthɑːt/
to take over /ˌteɪk 'əʊvə(r)/
villa /'vɪlə/
wedding anniversary
  /'wedɪŋ ˌænɪˌvɜːsəri/

Unit 8
Grammar
calcium /'kælsɪəm/
carbohydrate
  /ˌkɑːbəʊ'haɪdreɪt/
cash /kæʃ/
change /tʃeɪndʒ/
complex /'kɒmpleks/
diet /'daɪət/
fibre /'faɪbə(r)/
hip /hɪp/
to lose weight /ˌluːz 'weɪt/
mineral /'mɪnərəl/
to provide /prə'vaɪd/
thigh /θaɪ/
vitamin /'vɪtəmɪn/
Vocabulary
beef /biːf/
biscuits /'bɪskɪts/
breakfast cereal /'brekfəst
  ˌsɪərɪəl/
cabbage /'kæbɪdʒ/
cake /keɪk/
cod /kɒd/
grapes /greɪps/
margarine /ˌmɑːdʒə'riːn/
noodles /'nuːdlz/
nut /nʌt/
olive oil /ˌɒlɪv 'ɔɪl/
pork /pɔːk/
prawns /prɔːnz/
rice /raɪs/
salmon /'sæmən/
spaghetti /spə'geti/
sweets /swiːts/
tuna /'tjuːnə/
yoghurt /'jɒgət/
Reading
addiction /ə'dɪkʃn/
bar /bɑː(r)/
can (n) /kæn/
carton /'kɑːtn/
cocktail /'kɒkteɪl/
to cut down on /ˌkʌt 'daʊn ɒn/
doorway /'dɔːweɪ/
doughnut /'dəʊnʌt/
drugs /drʌgz/
to encourage /ɪŋ'kʌrɪdʒ/
enormous /ɪ'nɔːməs/

exercise /'eksəsaɪz/
exhausting /ɪg'zɔːstɪŋ/
to feed /fiːd/
fridge /frɪdʒ/
height /haɪt/
impressive /ɪm'presɪv/
incredible /ɪŋ'kredɪbl/
jar /dʒɑː(r)/
maximum /'mæksɪməm/
to move house /ˌmuːv 'haʊs/
overweight /ˌəʊvə'weɪt/
pot /pɒt/
prisoner /'prɪzənə(r)/
snack /snæk/
soft drink /ˌsɒft 'drɪŋk/
ton /tʌn/
tube /tjuːb/
to weigh /weɪ/
weight /weɪt/
Listening
(the) bill /bɪl/
dessert /dɪ'zɜːt/
French fries /ˌfrentʃ 'fraɪz/
house wine /ˌhaʊs 'waɪn/
jacket potato /ˌdʒækɪt
  pə'teɪtəʊ/
lamb chop /ˌlæm 'tʃɒp/
melon /'melən/
menu /'menjuː/
mineral water /'mɪnərəl
  ˌwɔːtə(r)/
receipt /rɪ'siːt/
sparkling /'spɑːklɪŋ/
still /stɪl/
Extension
add /æd/
based on /'beɪst ɒn/
to calculate /'kælkjʊˌleɪt/
degree /dɪ'griː/
heart disease /'hɑːt dɪˌziːz/
hereditary /hə'redətri/
inhabitant /ɪn'hæbɪtənt/
life expectancy /'laɪf
  ɪkˌspektənsi/
to lose your temper /ˌluːz
  jɔː 'tempə(r)/
partner /'pɑːtnə(r)/
postgraduate
  /ˌpəʊst'grædjʊət/
qualification /ˌkwɒlɪfɪ'keɪʃn/
questionnaire
  /ˌkwestʃə'neə(r)/
quick-tempered
  /ˌkwɪk 'tempəd/
rural /'rʊərəl/
sedentary /'sedəntri/
subtract /səb'trækt/
to suffer (from) /'sʌfə/
unhealthy /ʌn'helθi/
urban /'ɜːbən/

Unit 9
Grammar
to afford /ə'fɔːd/
charity /'tʃærəti/
circumstances
  /'sɜːkəmˌstɑːnsɪz/
to depend (on) /dɪ'pend/
emergency /ɪ'mɜːdʒənsi/
except /ɪk'sept/
fool /fuːl/
honest /'ɒnɪst/
ideal /aɪ'dɪəl/

to put back /ˌpʊt 'bæk/
wallet /'wɒlɪt/
Vocabulary
assault /ə'sɒlt/
blackmail /'blækmeɪl/
burglary /'bɜːgləri/
to kidnap /'kɪdnæp/
murder /'mɜːdə(r)/
robbery /'rɒbəri/
shoplifting /'ʃɒplɪftɪŋ/
vandalism /'vændəlɪzm/
Reading
apartment /ə'pɑːtmənt/
attitude /'ætɪtjuːd/
to cross the street /ˌkrɒs
  ðə 'striːt/
dial /'daɪəl/
extremely /ɪk'striːmli/
fire brigade /'faɪə brɪˌgeɪd/
to get involved /ˌget
  ɪn'vɒlvd/
hero /'hɪərəʊ/
to ignore /ɪg'nɔː(r)/
in flames /ɪn'fleɪmz/
to rescue /'reskjuː/
scream (n) /skriːm/
silly /'sɪli/
smoke (n) /sməʊk/
to stab /stæb/
stone /stəʊn/
to vandalize /'vændəlaɪz/
victim /'vɪktɪm/
witness /'wɪtnəs/
Listening
bottom /'bɒtəm/
to check in /ˌtʃek 'ɪn/
credit card /'kredɪt ˌkɑːd/
double /'dʌbl/
key /kiː/
registration form
  /ˌredʒɪ'streɪʃn ˌfɔːm/
to require /rɪ'kwaɪə(r)/
reservation /ˌrezə'veɪʃn/
to sign /saɪn/
Extension
advantage /əd'vɑːntɪdʒ/
alarm /ə'lɑːm/
to argue (with) /'ɑːgjuː/
bar code /'bɑː ˌkəʊd/
checkout /'tʃekaʊt/
disadvantage /ˌdɪsəd'vɑːntɪdʒ/
electronic /ˌɪlek'trɒnɪk/
guard /gɑːd/
to identify /aɪ'dentɪfaɪ/
power cut /'paʊə ˌkʌt/
purchase (n) /'pɜːtʃɪs/
queue /kjuː/
to replace /rɪ'pleɪs/
ring /rɪŋ/
to scan /skæn/
shelf /ʃelf/
slot /slɒt/
smart /smɑːt/
technician /tek'nɪʃn/
technology /tek'nɒlədʒi/
trolley /'trɒli/
to trust /trʌst/

Unit 10
Grammar
to give up /ˌgɪv 'ʌp/
to keep an eye on /ˌkiːp
  ən 'aɪ ɒn/

New Year's resolution
  /ˌnjuː jɪəz ˌrezə'luːʃn/
Vocabulary
activity /æk'tɪvəti/
to burn /bɜːn/
calories /'kæləriz/
energetic /enə'dʒetɪk/
moderate /'mɒdərət/
to rest /rest/
to shave /ʃeɪv/
to skate /skeɪt/
to skip /skɪp/
strenuous /'strenjʊəs/
to sunbathe /'sʌnbeɪð/
Reading
to appreciate /ə'priːʃɪeɪt/
to benefit /'benəfɪt/
civil engineer /ˌsɪvəl
  endʒɪ'nɪə(r)/
DIY /ˌdiː aɪ'waɪ/
to decline /dɪ'klaɪn/
demanding /dɪ'mɑːndɪŋ/
to deserve /dɪ'zɜːv/
dishwasher /'dɪʃˌwɒʃə(r)/
earnings /'ɜːnɪŋz/
full-time /ˌfʊl 'taɪm/
housewife /'haʊswaɪf/
housework /'haʊswɜːk/
part-time /ˌpɑːt 'taɪm/
practical /'præktɪkl/
researcher /rɪ'sɜːtʃə(r)/
to reveal /rɪ'viːl/
social worker /'səʊʃəl
  ˌwɜːkə(r)/
time-consuming /'taɪm
  kənˌsjuːmɪŋ/
value /'væljuː/
wages /'weɪdʒɪz/
workplace /'wɜːkpleɪs/
youngster /'jʌŋstə(r)/
Listening
to fancy /'fænsi/
to hire /'haɪə(r)/
to mind /maɪnd/
phone book /'fəʊn ˌbʊk/
picnic /'pɪknɪk/
serious /'sɪərɪəs/
Extension
to challenge /'tʃælɪndʒ/
crossword /'krɒswɜːd/
to daydream /'deɪdriːm/
everyday /'evrɪdeɪ/
massage /'mæsɑːʒ/
to meditate /'medɪteɪt/
outdoors /aʊt'dɔːz/
philosopher /fɪ'lɒsəfə(r)/
pleasure /'pleʒə(r)/
to pray /preɪ/
puzzle /'pʌzəl/
reaction /rɪ'ækʃn/
to redecorate /ˌriː'dekəreɪt/
religious service
  /rɪˌlɪdʒəs 'sɜːvɪs/
rock climbing /'rɒk ˌklaɪmɪŋ/
sky /skaɪ/
to socialize /'səʊʃəlaɪz/
to stimulate /'stɪmjʊleɪt/
survival /sə'vaɪvəl/

Unit 11
Grammar
audience /'ɔːdɪəns/
careful /'keəfl/

to chop down /ˌtʃɒp ˈdaʊn/
comfortable /ˈkʌmftəbl/
content (n) /ˈkɒntent/
fashion model /ˈfæʃn ˌmɒdl/
image /ˈɪmɪdʒ/
in the public eye /ɪn ðə ˌpʌblɪk ˈaɪ/
newsreader /ˈnjuːzˌriːdə(r)/
priest /priːst/
public life /ˌpʌblɪk ˈlaɪf/
royal /ˈrɔɪəl/

Vocabulary
DJ (disc jockey) /ˈdiː ˌdʒeɪ/
journalist /ˈdʒɜːnəlɪst/
presenter /prɪˈzentə(r)/
the news /ðəˈnjuːz/
weather presenter /ˈweðə prɪˌzentə(r)/

Reading
article /ˈɑːtɪkl/
artificial /ɑːtɪˈfɪʃl/
big business /ˌbɪg ˈbɪznɪs/
bright /braɪt/
consultant /kənˈsʌltənt/
to concentrate (on) /ˈkɒnsəntreɪt/
to criticise /ˈkrɪtɪsaɪz/
dull /dʌl/
to emphasize /ˈemfəsaɪz/
flattering /ˈflætərɪŋ/
to flirt /flɜːt/
front page /ˌfrʌnt ˈpeɪdʒ/
hairstyle /ˈheəstaɪl/
to identify with /aɪˈdentɪfaɪ wɪð/
lipstick /ˈlɪpstɪk/
to mention /ˈmenʃn/
neat /niːt/
to sack /sæk/
sexy /ˈseksi/
untidy /ʌnˈtaɪdi/
viewer /ˈvjuːə(r)/

Listening
caller /ˈkɔːlə(r)/
engaged /ɪŋˈgeɪdʒd/
extension /ɪkˈstenʃn/
to get through /ˌget ˈθruː/
to hang up /ˌhæŋ ˈʌp/
no reply /ˌnəʊ rɪˈplaɪ/
strange /streɪndʒ/
switchboard /ˈswɪtʃbɔːd/
to transfer /trænsˈfɜː/

Extension
arena /əˈriːnə/
bruise /bruːz/
chain /tʃeɪn/
to chase /tʃeɪs/
to climb up /ˌklaɪm ˈʌp/
competition /ˌkɒmpəˈtɪʃn/
contender /kənˈtendə(r)/
event /ɪˈvent/
gladiator /ˈglædɪeɪtə(r)/
gruelling /ˈgruːəlɪŋ/
to hang on /ˌhæŋ ˈɒn/
incredible /ɪŋˈkredɪbʊl/
to knock off /ˌnɒk ˈɒf/
obstacle /ˈɒbstəkl/
platform /ˈplætfɔːm/
to pull off /ˌpʊl ˈɒf/
to race /reɪs/
ring /rɪŋ/
to store /skɔː(r)/
stick /stɪk/

to swing /swɪŋ/

Unit 12
Grammar
to abandon /əˈbændən/
astronaut /ˈæstrənɔːt/
atmosphere /ˈætməsfɪə(r)/
to burn /bɜːn/
to collect /kəˈlekt/
debris /ˈdeɪbriː/
fragment /ˈfrægmənt/
glove /glʌv/
to head (towards) /hed/
to launch /lɔːntʃ/
object /ˈɒbdʒekt/
orbit /ˈɔːbɪt/
to pollute /pəˈluːt/
rubbish /ˈrʌbɪʃ/
satellite /ˈsætəlaɪt/
to scatter /ˈskætə(r)/
space /speɪs/
space station /speɪs ˌsteɪʃən/
spacecraft /ˈspeɪskrɑːft/
spanner /ˈspænə(r)/

Vocabulary
comet /ˈkɒmɪt/
continent /ˈkɒntɪnənt/
desert /ˈdezət/
hemisphere /ˈhemɪsfɪə(r)/
island /ˈaɪlənd/
moon /muːn/
North Pole /ˌnɔːθ ˈpəʊl/
ocean /ˈəʊʃən/
peninsula /pəˈnɪnsjʊlə/
solar system /ˌsəʊlə ˌsɪstəm/
volcano /vɒlˈkeɪnəʊ/

Reading
to boil /bɔɪl/
chaos /ˈkeɪɒs/
civilization /ˌsɪvəlaɪˈzeɪʃn/
cloud /klaʊd/
to collapse /kəˈlæps/
crop /krɒp/
dinosaur /ˈdaɪnəsɔː(r)/
to drown /draʊn/
dust /dʌst/
to evacuate /ɪˈvækjuːeɪt/
explosion /ɪkˈspləʊʒn/
(to become) extinct /ɪkˈstɪŋkt/
massive /ˈmæsɪv/
outwards /ˈaʊtwədz/
to ruin /ˈruːɪn/
sea bed /ˈsiː bed/
to set off /ˌset ˈɒf/
shock wave /ˈʃɒk weɪv/
to spread /spred/
temperature /ˈtemprətʃə(r)/
tidal wave /ˈtaɪdəl weɪv/
war (to break out) /wɔː(r)/

Listening
Christmas /ˈkrɪsməs/
congratulations /kənˌgrætjʊˈleɪʃnz/
driving test /ˈdraɪvɪŋ ˌtest/
due /djuː/
medal /ˈmedl/
nil /nɪl/
to split up /ˌsplɪt ˈʌp/

Extension
to accept /əkˈsept/
carat /ˈkærət/
coin /kɔɪn/

to commit a crime /kəˌmɪt ə ˈkraɪm/
earring /ˈɪərɪŋ/
empire /ˈempaɪə(r)/
fascinated /ˈfæsəneɪtɪd/
government /ˈgʌvənmənt/
individual /ˌɪndɪˈvɪdjʊəl/
industry /ˈɪndəstri/
jungle /ˈdʒʌŋgl/
metal /ˈmetl/
military /ˈmɪlətri/
to mix (with) /mɪks/
nugget /ˈnʌgət/
outlaw /ˈaʊtlɔː/
pure /pjʊə(r)/
reserve /rɪˈzɜːv/
sailor /ˈseɪlə(r)/
seed /siːd/
shipwrecked /ˈʃɪprekt/
tomb /tuːm/

Unit 13
Grammar
amnesia /æmˈniːziə/
car crash /ˈkɑː ˌkræʃ/
compact disc /ˌkɒmpækt ˈdɪsk/
dramatically /drəˈmætɪkli/
to erase /ɪˈreɪz/
to invent /ɪnˈvent/
laboratory /ləˈbɒrətri/
lead singer /ˌliːd ˈsɪŋə(r)/
memory /ˈmeməri/
microwave (oven) /ˈmaɪkrəʊweɪv/
pop group /ˈpɒp ˌgruːp/
prime minister /ˌpraɪm ˈmɪnɪstə(r)/
teenager /ˈtiːneɪdʒə(r)/
word processor /ˌwɜːd ˈprəʊsesə(r)/

Vocabulary
century /ˈsentʃəri/
decade /ˈdekeɪd/
season /ˈsiːzn/
second /ˈsekənd/

Reading
to affect /əˈfekt/
as a result /ˌəz ə rɪˈzʌlt/
cave /keɪv/
constant /ˈkɒnstənt/
decorator /ˈdekəreɪtə(r)/
depressed /dɪˈprest/
entertainment /ˌentəˈteɪnmənt/
experiment /ɪkˈsperɪmənt/
link /lɪŋk/
living quarters /ˈlɪvɪŋ ˌkwɔːtəz/
mental /ˈmentl/
physical /ˈfɪzɪkl/
to play cards /ˌpleɪ ˈkɑːdz/
rhythm /ˈrɪðəm/
tape /teɪp/
underground /ˌʌndəˈgraʊnd/
volunteer /ˌvɒlənˈtɪə(r)/

Listening
available /əˈveɪləbl/
check-up /ˈtʃek ʌp/
flight times /ˈflaɪt ˌtaɪmz/
fully booked /ˌfʊli ˈbʊkt/
nothing left /ˌnʌθɪŋ ˈleft/
otherwise /ˈʌðəwaɪz/
seat /siːt/

Extension
bad-tempered /ˌbæd ˈtempəd/
barn /bɑːn/
battle /ˈbætl/
to claim /kleɪm/
court /kɔːt/
to hang /hæŋ/
helpful /ˈhelpfl/
in order to /ɪn ˈɔːdə tə/
inheritance /ɪnˈherɪtəns/
judge /dʒʌdʒ/
pleasant /ˈpleznt/
secretly /ˈsiːkrətli/
soldier /ˈsəʊldʒə(r)/
to treat (well/badly) /triːt/
trial /ˈtraɪəl/
to unite /juːˈnaɪt/
wooden /ˈwʊdn/
to wound /wuːnd/

Unit 14
Grammar
amazed /əˈmeɪzd/
to apply (to) /əˈplaɪ tə/
gym /dʒɪm/
to have a word with /ˌhæv ə ˈwɜːd wɪð/
to manage /ˈmænɪdʒ/
personal /ˈpɜːsənl/
professional /prəˈfeʃnəl/
slogan /ˈsləʊgən/
system /ˈsɪstəm/
trivial /ˈtrɪvɪəl/
to type /taɪp/

Vocabulary
respected /rɪˈspektɪd/
selfish /ˈselfɪʃ/
thrilling /ˈθrɪlɪŋ/

Reading
club /klʌb/
correspondent /ˌkɒrɪˈspɒndənt/
crisis /ˈkraɪsɪs/
excitement /ɪkˈsaɪtmənt/
exclusive /ɪkˈskluːsɪv/
feeling /ˈfiːlɪŋ/
foreign /ˈfɒrən/
God /gɒd/
lucky charm /ˌlʌki ˈtʃɑːm/
masochist /ˈmæsəkɪst/
opportunity /ˌɒpəˈtjuːnəti/
organization /ˌɔːgənaɪˈzeɪʃn/
to promise /ˈprɒmɪs/
screen /skriːn/
shell /ʃel/
to shoot /ʃuːt/
the front line /ðə ˌfrʌnt ˈlaɪn/
thrill /θrɪl/

Listening
grey /greɪ/
run (n) /rʌn/
whereabouts /ˈweərəbaʊts/

Extension
blues /bluːz/
congressman /ˈkɒŋgresmən/
cure /kjʊə(r)/
fuss /fʌs/
sick /sɪk/
the United Nations /ðə juːˌnaɪtɪd ˈneɪʃnz/
vacation /veɪˈkeɪʃn/
to vote /vəʊt/

OXFORD
UNIVERSITY PRESS

Great Clarendon Street, Oxford OX2 6DP

Oxford University Press is a department of the University of Oxford.
It furthers the University's objective of excellence in research, scholarship,
and education by publishing worldwide in

Oxford New York

Auckland Cape Town Dar es Salaam Hong Kong Karachi
Kuala Lumpur Madrid Melbourne Mexico City Nairobi
New Delhi Shanghai Taipei Toronto

With offices in

Argentina Austria Brazil Chile Czech Republic France Greece
Guatemala Hungary Italy Japan Poland Portugal Singapore
South Korea Switzerland Thailand Turkey Ukraine Vietnam

OXFORD and OXFORD ENGLISH are registered trade marks of
Oxford University Press in the UK and in certain other countries

ACKNOWLEDGEMENTS

The author would especially like to record his gratitude to his wife, Eunice,
and his children, without whose support and patience Lifelines would not
have been written. The author would also like to thank all those at Oxford
University Press who have contributed their skills and ideas to producing
this book

*The publisher and author are very grateful to the following teachers and institutions
for reading and/or piloting the manuscript and for providing invaluable comment and
feedback on the course:* Etienne André and Yolaine Sebaoun (CCI Nice, France),
Nicolo Arcadipane, Freda Miller, Judy Edwards and Barbara Ann Nutt
(International House, Marilla-Banditella, Italy), Éva Berényi and Erika Áipli
(Coventry House, Kecskemét, Hungary), Mary Boyd (The British Council,
Bologna, Italy), John Bryant and Lindsay McLellan (British Institute,
Valencia, Spain), Debbie Derrick and Madeleine Kear (Scanbrit School of
English, Bournemouth, UK), Sarah Hunter and Stephen Yates (Colchester
English Study Centre, UK), Amanda Jeffries (Regent Oxford, UK), Heather
Jones (freelance, UK), Paula Jullian and Ana Maria Burdoch (Universidad de
los Andes, Santiago, Chile), Rita Lendvai, Dorottya Nagy and Philip Wood
(Atalanta International, Budapest, Hungary), Frances Lowndes (freelance,
UK), Edward Marten (CLM Bell School, Bolzano, Italy), Pamela Murphy
(freelance, UK), S. Mutter, Fiona McEwan-Cox and Julie Anne Maynard (The
British School, Verona, Italy), Cristina Nogueira and Kathryn Chown
(Cultura Inglesa, Rio de Janeiro, Brazil), Jesus M. Signes and Sarah-Louise
Scotney (Lingua International, Badalona, Spain), Professor Manja Strubej
and Tatjana Bleiweis (Izobrazevalno Sredisce Mikosic, Ljubljana, Slovenia),
Kiss Tibor, Laura Mitchell, Paluska Tünde and David Lewis (International
Language School, Nyiregyhaza, Hungary), Eszter Timár and Judit Kovács
(Bell Schools, Budapest, Hungary), Katalin Vizi (Lingua School of English,
Budapest, Hungary)

*The author and publishers would like to thank the following for permission to
reproduce their photographs:* A. A. & A. Ancient Art and Architecture Collection
(42), Ace Photo Agency (76), Aspect Picture Library Ltd (103), BBC Picture
Archives (115), Barnaby's Picture Library (62), Corbis/Bettman (26, 118),
Coca-Cola Great Britain & Ireland (15), Philip Dunn Picture Library (68), Eye
Ubiquitous (87, 92, 103), Sally and Richard Greenhill (18, 58, 108), Oliver
Hutton (22, 23), ITN (91), The Image Bank (6, 13, 15, 18, 21, 42, 56, 59, 100,
101), Katz Pictures Ltd (11, 88), The Kobal Collection Ltd (42), London
Weekend Television (94, 95), Frances Lowndes (28, 29), Network
Photographers Ltd (87, 89), Popperfoto (115), Powerstock Photo Library
(13, 58, 62, 75, 84, 87), Rex Features Ltd (10, 11, 66), Ross Parry Picture
Agency (24), Jeffrey L Rotman/Photography (30), Science Photo Library Ltd
(96, 97), Frank Spooner Pictures Ltd (66, 88, 107), Tony Stone Images (15, 18,
20, 28, 29, 31, 43, 51, 56, 62, 72, 75, 87, 100, 103), Sygma Ltd (88, 110, 111),
TRIP (15, 56, 62, 75), Telegraph Colour Library (15, 32, 35, 62, 118),
Viewfinder Colour Photo Library Ltd (13, 18, 75, 92), Sylvia Wheeldon and
Tim Falla (58)

We would also like to thank: ABC Taxis (Oxford), BBC Thames Valley FM,
Heathrow Airport Limited, Hobbs Limited, staff at the Oxford Playhouse, and
the Randolph Hotel, Oxford for their help with location photography

Commissioned photography by: Paul Freestone (8, 9, 25, 45, 55, 60, 61, 100, 108,
112, 116); Mark Mason (12, 20, 36, 105)

Picture research by: Mandy Twells

Illustrations by: Adrian Barclay (78, 79), Katherine Baxter (16), Rupert Besley
(7, 80), Ian Dicks (41, 48, 49, 70, 71, 96), Paul Fisher-Johnson (39), Neil
Gower (12, 52, 53, 67), Conny Jude (44, 83), Joanna Kerr (40, 83, 84), Angela
Salt (46), Raymond Turvey (30, 42, 98, 107)

Songs: You've got what it takes (Gordy/Gordy/Davis) © 1959 Jobete Music Co
Inc. and *California Dreaming* (Phillips/Phillips) Reproduced by kind
permission, MCA MUSIC LTD *Summertime Blues* (Capehart/Cochran) © 1958
Warner-Tamerlane Publishing Corp., Rightsong Music, Elvis Presley Music &
Gladys Music, Cinephonic Music Co Ltd., 8/9 Frith Street, London W1V 5TZ

*The publisher and author are grateful to those who have given permission to reproduce
the following extracts and adaptations of copyright material:* p 6 Reproduced by
kind permission of The Automobile Association; pp 24, 25 Extracts from
'The Gretna Grapple' by John Woodcock and 'Together at last, couple
dogged by a pet hatred' by James Grylls, The Daily Mail © The Daily
Mail/Solo Syndications by permission; pp 26, 27 Reproduced by permission
of The Reader's Digest Association Limited from 'Marvels and Mysteries of
the Human Mind' © 1992; p 31 Adapted from 'Shark Attack!' by Mary M.
Cerullo © Focus; p 35 Extract from 'Whites will soon be a minority race in
America' by George Gordon in The Daily Mail © The Daily Mail/Solo
Syndications by permission; p 51 Adapted from brochure 'Inspirations
Nepal' by kind permission of CVA Media Ltd; p 66 Extract taken from 'Can
you Imagine Weighing 100 Stone?' by Simon Kinnersley, Woman's Own by
permission; p78 From 'Smart store threat to girls on the checkouts' by Sean
Poulter, The Daily Mail © The Daily Mail/Solo Syndications by permission;
p 82 Reproduced from 'Burn off that excess baggage' © Lindsay Nicholson/
The Daily Telegraph plc, London, 1991; p 83 Extract from 'The £349
Housewife' by Sean Poulter, The Daily Mail © The Daily Mail/Solo
Syndications by permission; pp 86, 87 Adapted from 'Pleasure Principle' by
Jerome Burne, © Focus; p 90 Extract from 'How they gave Fiona that certain
something' by Rebecca Hardy, The Daily Mail © The Daily Mail/Solo
Syndications by permission; p 91 Extract from 'How I was floored by the
F-factor' by Fiona Armstrong, The Daily Mail by permission; p 90 Extracts
from 'Slapping Dallas Gloss on an Outdoor Girl' by Lyndia Lee-Potter; p 102
'The New Gold Rush' by Paul Harris; p 104 'The Forgotten Years' by James
Grylls, The Daily Mail © The Daily Mail/Solo Syndications by permission;
p 99 Adapted from 'Horror that ends history if a comet hits the earth'
© Focus; p 107 Reproduced by permission of The Reader's Digest Assocation
Limited from 'Marvels and Mysteries of the Human Mind' © 1992

Although every effort has been made to trace and contact copyright holders
before publication, this has not been possible in some cases. We apologize
for any apparent infringement of copyright and if notified, the publisher
will be pleased to rectify any errors or omissions at the earliest opportunity

*The author and publishers would like to thank the following for permission to
reproduce their material:* EMI Records (UK) (105), The Oldie Book of Cartoons,
published by Park McDonald Books 1995, edited & selected by Richard
Ingrams (13, 50, 69, 109, 119), The Spectator Cartoon Book 1994 (53, 94)